Pond Business

How to Succeed Across the Atlantic

Mark Sutherland

ISBN 978-1-949718-02-7

DUNROBIN
PUBLISHING

www.dunrobin.us

Praise for Pond Business

"Mark's book is an important tool for transatlantic business folks to help them build economic relationships which will endure and will remain 'special.'"

Ambassador Steve Bridges

"For companies looking at building a transatlantic presence, this book is a valuable read. It is full of actionable insights and experienced perspectives that today's business leaders in the UK and US can use to launch into the other country in a way that will help increase success and reduce risk. I thoroughly recommend Pond Business *for anyone looking to build business links between our two countries."*

Consul General John Saville

*"*Pond Business *is a short, insightful and useful read for UK/US executives wanting to do business in the other's country."*

Simon Constable
Fellow at Johns Hopkins Institute
Author, Broadcaster, Commentator, Speaker

"In today's social media driven society, one where we are constantly reminded that we are all part of a global village, it is all too easy to assume that barriers to effective and meaningful business relationships can be readily overcome. After all, we know what we mean don't we? Mark's book effectively dispels that myth: we might think we know each other but the reality is much more nuanced. The helpful pointers in this book act as an essential toolkit for any business person seeking to make the right impression right from the start. And that's when it matters most. This book provides a unique and essential guide for businesses on how to invest, nurture relationships and flourish in the USA and UK."

Donnie Jack
Scotland's Senior Diplomat in North America, 2014-16

"If you are planning to do business in the UK, this is a must read. From practical insights to cultural perspectives and team suggestions, Pond Business *is your essential guidebook to building the necessary connections with your cousins across the Atlantic."*

Steve Johnson
CEO, St. Louis Regional Economic Development Alliance

"Mark Sutherland is a consummate professional with an amazing talent for organizing information and directing people to the resources to accomplish their goals. As one who has worked with him politically, professionally and personally for two decades, I can highly recommend the wisdom in these pages."

Senator John Loudon (Ret.)
President, Gonzalez Family Office

TABLE OF CONTENTS

To the many public servants
who are underpaid and unrecognized
and who have dedicated their lives
to protecting and growing the
special relationship between
the UK and the USA.

It's certainly a team sport.

Thank you for your sacrifices
and your dedication.

Foreword by

The Rt Hon The Lord Swraj Paul, Privy Counsellor

and Ambassador Steve Bridges, LVO

~

Lord Paul

Born in India, I first came to the US in 1949 to study mechanical engineering at the Massachusetts Institute of Technology (MIT). Since then, I have always retained an affection for America, and my children have been educated there. In the late 1960's I came to Britain, have lived here ever since and have been a British citizen for many years.

Throughout my business life I have dealt with the US, whether buying, selling or investing, and my UK-based company Caparo now has manufacturing plants across the

US in Chicago IL, Gerald MO, Elkhart IN, Trenton GA, Masury OH, Case Grande AZ, and Manchester IA, all of which we have chosen to headquarter in St Louis, MO.

At this time of great change for Britain, as it prepares to leave the shelter of the European Union, I have looked back over the last 65 years of my life as to what may encourage those active in business in these two great nations to further their commercial engagement in the future, based on my own personal experience.

While we think we speak the same language, in reality there are many differences between the two nations. Yet there remains enormous affection between the peoples of these two countries and, like myself, many of the residents of both countries share a common history and cultural influences.

If we are to build on our collective experience, and to strengthen our commercial partnerships, then may I set out a few observations.

I have worked in many countries during my life, and I have always found that a key to success is trying to understand how the other person thinks and lives, and what matters to him or her. Put yourself in the other person's shoes, listen to what they have to say, observe and respect their customs, and show humility. Only then will you have the chance to gain his or her trust and do more together.

Go and meet people. It is all too easy in this modern age to hide behind the desk and the screen and the data we all produce. You will only learn about each other by sitting down and discussing things, whether across the meeting room table or over a cup of coffee.

Always talk to your workforce, not just the people at the top; they know more than you might think, and you'll be able to sense the mood of the team.

Your way may not be the only way—be receptive to others' ideas and think first before you impose 'the corporate vision' on others as to whether it will work.

Listen, observe and, above all, don't lose your sense of humour!

***

Ambassador Bridges

George Bernard Shaw was once reported to have said that the UK and USA were "two nations divided by a common language!" Having lived in the USA for the past 6 years or so and having spent three decades before that as a British Diplomat and Ambassador working closely with my American friends and colleagues across the globe, I can relate to Shaw's quip.

There is so much that is familiar about the US for us Brits, which probably explains why over a million of us visit Florida alone every year and about half a million actually live there! And the reverse is true for Americans visiting the United Kingdom, even if we do drive on the opposite side of the road!

The UK and USA are very close friends. I will leave others to determine whether our relationship is still as "special" as Winston Churchill believed in 1946. But whatever term we use, there is no doubting that our two nations pride themselves on sharing what President Obama deemed an "important" bond. If we consider defence and intelligence, investment and trade and business, culture and movies and television, and a commonality of interests and values, then Britain and America remain hugely important for each other, and there are perhaps no two nations on earth that cooperate with such breadth and depth.

This is evident in our economic ties. When serving as the UK Government's senior representative for the Midwest USA based in Chicago, I would often pose the question both to UK and US citizens asking, "Which country is the largest foreign investor or largest foreign employer in USA, or for that matter in the UK?" The normal response would be China or Japan or Germany. "Wrong," I would reply. The UK is by far the largest foreign investor in the USA, just as the US is the largest in the UK. A million Brits work for US companies in the UK and the same number work for Brit companies across the Unites States. The USA is also the UK's single largest trading partner.

But now this is where it gets complicated. These close ties and this comfortable relationship can often lead to complacency and not just in language. "To luck out" in the USA is the equivalent for instance of "you're in luck" in UK. There are many other examples which can endorse Shaw's linguistic conclusion. For all our similarities and bonds of friendship, the UK and the USA are very different places and, in some ways, can appear as "foreign" to each other as nations in the "mystic orient." I could cite examples of how UK companies have struggled to succeed in the USA because they misunderstood local tax or labour laws—and "yes" just about every US State has its own local tax rates etc. The States may be United as a nation, but they are anything but in terms of their local business practices. Just as this huge nation requires us to use a GPS (US) or SatNav (UK) to help us small island folks get around, so we need a GPS to help us navigate the back roads of business practice. And as always, the reverse is so for American companies looking to do business in the UK. Never underestimate the size of the USA—it is huge both in terms of sheer geography and the time needed to get from one side to the other—but also the scale of individual States' economies; Missouri for instance, where the author, Mark Sutherland, and his family live, has an economy similar in size to the Philippines; Illinois to the north is comparable to Saudi Arabia, while the whole of the Midwest is the geographical equivalent of Western Europe with an economy bigger than Germany. The USA is a big place and it has regional disparities; just as we do in the UK.

"Know before you go" is extremely resonant advice for all business folks looking to explore UK or US markets. All of which is perhaps a typically British Diplomatic way of saying, that my good friend Mark's book is an important tool for transatlantic business folks to help them build economic relationships which will endure and will remain "special."

Introduction

This is a book that has been 30 years in the making. Ever since immigrating to the US from the UK, I have been driven by a desire for others to see the opportunities that exist a short hop across the Atlantic, or The Pond as I and many others refer to it.

These opportunities are many. They are economic, they are diplomatic, they are cultural, educational, research-inal … you get the point, I hope. I am fully convinced that to access Europe, even post-Brexit, the United Kingdom is the best place for a US company to look to for setting up shop or trading. I am also fully convinced that the trade relationship between the UK and the US can be, and will be, stronger than ever in the future. Even in the midst of what has been a rather dynamic and shifting Brexit debate, Britain continues to be one of the strongest economies in Europe. My encouragement as you look at the seemingly chaotic scenes in Parliament is to also realize that the UK is one of the strongest performing economies in Europe and that in the midst of Brexit drama, the UK is seeing incredibly high levels of foreign investment.

I am also fully convinced that British companies looking to continue Britain's global business leadership should look to the US, and the Midwest specifically, as their gateway to North America. The US, for the past seven years, has been the place where the world's global business leaders want to invest and grow according to the A.T. Kearney annual FDI Confidence Index. The UK, as an aside, has been ranked at number four in the world for the past three years, despite the uncertainty that has come with the Brexit negotiations.

And I would contend, maybe controversially, that the Trump administration may be one of the best times for UK companies to invest in the US due to the President's affinity for the UK, his support for increased trade and investment, and his predictability. Yes, predictability.

President Trump, when you look at him through the lens of internationalism as defined by Lady Thatcher in her

Downing Street Years autobiography, is committed to acting in what he defines as the best interests of his country. And knowing where he is coming from, makes it easier to make business decisions that can benefit from the current administration's plans and actions. He is focused on America first, rather than globalism first. And he seems to be working down his list of campaign promises in order to fulfill them. With that in mind, regardless of your view of the politics involved, you can come to pretty good conclusions about where he wishes to take things and make educated decisions as to where the business opportunities may lie.

Add to that the Global Economic Policy Uncertainty Index I will discuss further in the final chapter of this book, and the UK and the US both look incredibly attractive today.

This book's entire purpose is to start you on your journey of Pond-crossing business. It's not an in-depth tome with all the necessary legal guidance on how to run a multi-national company. It is simply a guide book, kind of like a tourist guide for your business dealings.

The content comes from 30 years of interesting cross-Pond interactions. Being involved in economic development, marketing, international diplomacy, and cultural promotion has given me a perspective that has caused me to find the good in both the US and the UK. And it's also created some amusing circumstances over the years that I hope you can learn from.

My hope is that this book is informative, slightly entertaining, and a valuable tool as you look at expansion or trade with the other country. And beyond these pages, if there is anything else I can assist you with, regardless of whether you are looking east or west, please do not hesitate to reach out.

Together, we can make the special relationship between our two countries the most powerful economic and trading relationship of the 21st century.

Mark Sutherland
St. Louis, Missouri, USA

Pond Business

How to Succeed Across the Atlantic

Chapter 1

Two Countries Separated by a Common Language

When I first came to America in 1989, I was met by many interesting and memorable questions. Deep questions of such an esoteric nature that it caused you to pause and contemplate deeply before answering. Brilliant questions such as "Did you drive here?" and "Do they have radios in England?" plus "Isn't that near Canada?" and my absolute favorite, "What language do they speak in England?"

Thankfully those stunning questions were asked by the minority of Yanks, but it did drive home for me the fact that Americans, as a whole, don't know much about the UK. And vice versa, I knew little to nothing about the US. My only knowledge of the US, and Missouri where I settled, before setting foot in America was a stunning plethora of educational information as found on the A-Team, the Dukes of Hazard, the television show Dallas, and a travel show on BBC2 that introduced British audiences to St. Louis, Missouri, as the home of brain sandwiches, frozen custard, Budweiser, a big Arch, theme parks, and gospel singers on local television broadcasting from their furniture store.

Both my perspective and the perspectives of the first Americans I met were nowhere near reality. This has thankfully improved over the decades since, especially in my adopted home town of St. Louis, Missouri, which has become quite an international city with many flavors from all over the world—including the UK.

But what is real is that sometimes the communication between a Yank and a Brit can still be completely full of misunderstandings or false assumptions—due to the very words used. We hear them, and think we are speaking the same language. The words used in either country and culture sound similar, most of the time, but the meaning behind them should never be assumed. Because sometimes, just sometimes, they don't mean what you think they mean.

Also, a word of warning Brits. Slow down and finish your words. I had one friend tell me it took about two years for him to understand a word I said, and that most of the time he was just smiling and nodding while comprehending nothing. Does wonders for the ego when you are told, however nicely, that you are nonsensical to your mates—and that's prior to any liquid influence on said fluency.

And don't even consider trying to order a water at a drive-thru window, or anywhere else for that matter. I have lost count of the number of times I have said the word water numerous times and finally have to revert to $H2O$ in order for them to actually understand the word I am using. My only fear is that one day people won't study science anymore, then have no idea what $H2O$ is, and I die of thirst as a result. But there's always rum I suppose. But I digress.

In the 1940s, Irish playwright George Bernard Shaw was reported as stating that the United States and Great Britain are two countries separated by a common language. Any of us who have been in both countries know that this was a genius statement proven out in every single interaction we have in the other country, sometimes leaving us with humorous stories to tell. And while Sir Winston Churchill gave us hope by stating in 1943 during a speech at Harvard University in Cambridge, Massachusetts, that "the gift of a common tongue is a priceless inheritance and it may well someday become the foundation of a common citizenship," and he even built upon that thought during his 1946 speech in Fulton, Missouri, where he first used the term "special relationship" to describe the friendship our two nations enjoy, it is—with many apologies to the former Prime Minister—much safer to defer to Shaw over Sir Winston. Especially if you are considering anything more than an informal transatlantic connection.

Just a quick look at a dictionary from the other country will give you thousands of words that either have different meanings in either country or that only actually exist in one nation and would be met with blank stares in the other.

Frustrated much?

For example, imagine you are sitting in a hotel in the opposing nation considering taking in that fun and memorable experience of a live musical. You, of course, check out the reviews, which describe said show as "a bomb." Depending on which nation you find yourself in, you are either depressed or excited. And quite possibly, you are having the exact opposite reaction than was intended by the word used. The meaning of "a bomb" in this case is the complete opposite depending on which nation you find yourself in. In the UK, if reading about the latest opus in the

West End of London, a bomb means the show is a great success. However, a bomb on New York's Broadway is a complete disaster of a show, and one on which you shouldn't waste your time or money.

So, not quite sure how to proceed, you instead decide to go shopping to part with your money. But again, here confusion reigns. You get a ride to the store in the US, but a lift to the shops in the UK. You push a trolley in the UK but push a cart in the US. Jam and jelly are opposites, sometimes but not always. Biscuits are not the same in the other nation as British biscuits are US cookies, and US biscuits are like savory UK scones. UK sweets are US candy, US chips are UK crisps and UK chips are US French fries. And don't even get started on carbonated drinks. Not even Americans can agree on what to call them so depending on where you are in the US you may be asking for soda, or pop, or Coke, or fizz, or who the heck knows what else. You might get so flustered, you'll try to cross the road, look the wrong way, and get narrowly missed by a truck, or a lorry if you happen to be in the UK. Then you just might have soiled your pants (in the UK) or underwear (in the US), or at least fallen over and dirtied your trousers (in the UK) or pants (in the US).

So now your pants/trousers are dirty, you head to your first-floor apartment (US) or flat (UK) to change into a nice clean sweater (US) or jumper (UK) and eat some fries (US) or chips (UK) or chips (US) or crisps (UK) and maybe a cookie (US) or biscuit (UK). But can you find your first-floor apartment? If you are in the US, that means it's on the ground floor. If you are in the UK, it's on the floor above the ground floor.

Confused yet?

And I haven't even opened the Pandora's box of grammar rules! In the US, people are quite comfortable turning nouns into verbs, and verbs and nouns into adjectives. In Britain, disrespect for grammatical rules is just not done among the older generation, although among the younger generation it is much more common. And tenses are different, plurals are treated differently, and collective nouns will drive you batty.

It might actually be worthwhile for a Brit to invest time in watching American sitcoms or movies and for an American to invest some time in watching The Crown or various other British television shows in order to get more comfortable with the language from the other side. After all, what American doesn't want to understand and correctly use power words and phrases such as twit, namby-pamby, shambles, give a fig, mollycoddle, and gung-ho.

Let us be completely and utterly blunt. The biggest mistake you can make as an international businessperson, is to assume that because both the US and the UK speak "English," that doing business in the UK as an American, and vice versa, is going to be culturally and experientially identical to your experience in your native country. It is not. It will not be. And you had better be prepared to prep and plan and maybe even hire a "translator." Many a business arrangement has been ruined by a lack of cultural awareness and cultural sensitivity, and even basic language skills, that are essential to good business relations in any country. You must understand that, and you must constantly keep aware of, you, as a Yank in King Arthur's Court, are not in Kansas, or Missouri, or even that strange area of America known as California anymore. And you, as the latest iteration of the British Invasion, can make it a really Hard Day's Night if you are not careful.

The key things to remember as you get started on your transatlantic adventure is each country has its own distinct language and words and you shouldn't assume British English and American English are the same.

Also, do your research. Take the time to learn about the other country and the culture within, which can mean watching the telly (UK) or TV (US) for "research purposes" and basically have fun learning just how amazing the other country is.

Chapter 2

Cultural Differences

Ricky Gervais, the British award-winning comedian, wrote a rather interesting article for *Time* in November 2011 that gives us a wee bit of insight into the cultural differences between the UK and the USA.

"It's often dangerous to generalize, but under threat, I would say that Americans are more 'down the line,'" he wrote. "[Americans] don't hide their hopes and fears. They applaud ambition and openly reward success. Brits are more comfortable with life's losers. We embrace the underdog until it's no longer the underdog. We like to bring authority down a peg or two. Americans say, 'Have a nice day' whether they mean it or not. Brits are terrified to say this."

And thus we begin to understand that our two nations are full of people who act, think and view the world differently from each other. However, because we seem to look the same on the outside due to our style of dress or culture, and speak a similar language, we can very easily fall into the dangerous assumption that we think the same way in life and in business. And a failure to understand this can be costly indeed.

"I think the key things here would be small differences in terms of surfacing ambiguities and getting down to the nitty gritty of deal-making," a friend of mine in the UK's Department of International Trade (DIT) told me once. "It's a little bit of a cliché but true all the same that Brits can have slightly less focused pitches and be a bit reticent about explaining what they are really good at and why their product or service is the best." Basically, Brits don't like to brag, even when their boasts are absolutely true.

"The other area I find is in terms of selling yourself individually," he continued. "Americans can sometimes be a bit more upfront about where they went to school, where they live, even what they earn, whereas for some Brits a kind of modesty can prevail."

Another friend, this one at Scottish Development International (SDI), discussed with me the differences between Scotland and the US.

"They are two countries that have a lot in common beneath it all, but do not downplay the differences," he said. "Learn to genuinely appreciate what makes each country unique, from both a personal and business perspective."

And that mutual appreciation can go a long way to building solid connections that thrive across the Pond. A few years back I wrote on occasion for the Weekly Telegraph on expat issues and had the pleasure of introducing the UK readers to some fascinating and fun connections between the UK and Missouri.

While writing for the Telegraph, I covered the UK Government's pop-up consulate in Kansas City, Missouri, where the entire Chicago consulate team spent a week in KC hosting events and building connections with the region, the businesses and the leadership. Events held ranged from a moving tribute to our heroes in uniform at the World War I Museum, to a Missouri-based Beatles Tribute Band, Liverpool Legends, who performed to a large crowd in downtown Kansas City.

I also used a photo of myself in the article with my arm around a cardboard cutout of a certain prominent British leader, which unfortunately resulted in those cardboard cutouts never being used again. Apparently, one does not do such things.

In other articles, I covered a visit to St. Louis by my good friend Donnie Jack, who at the time was the senior diplomat from Scotland in North America. On the baseball field underneath the St. Louis Arch, St. Louis presented him with a St. Louis Cardinal's shirt with Scotland and 2014 emblazoned across the back. And hundreds of people turned out to an event with Donnie at St. Louis University to hear the latest on opportunities to move Scotland and Missouri closer together.

I had the opportunity to highlight these British invasions and use them to raise awareness of the great opportunities that exist to build all sorts of connections between the United Kingdom and the United States, and Missouri in particular.

Another element in the cultural differences is the use of language. For example, if you are off playing golf in the UK and the marshal comes along, all pleasant and friendly, and suggests that you may want to pick it up a bit, just a pace, in a jovial sort of way, and then wanders off—you had better take heed. What he really meant was you had better kick it up big time because you are playing way too slow. If he comes back again and you haven't sped up a lot, the subtlety will no longer be there, and you will certainly hear rather directly just how slow you are.

You have also a need to set aside your pre-conceived ideas about the other country. As my DIT friend puts it, "US companies assume that in the UK it rains all the time and we have terrible food (neither are true) and that London is the sole place of interest (it is not). And UK companies looking at the US are often under-estimating its scale and the fact that it is multiple big markets—not just New York, Chicago and Los Angeles. And assumptions about politics can be a little simplistic."

So, now that it's been brought up, what about politics? Should you bring them up in polite conversation? Is it a "safe topic?" And can you assume you know the political persuasion of the person you are talking to?

I think the answer to all three is a no if you want to be completely and utterly safe (and boring). But, just for the sake of adventure and curiosity, what if you really, really, really wanted to talk politics?

A good example is my recent experience in Covent Garden, sitting outside The Salisbury, enjoying a London Pride and some delicious appetizers. It's a smashing wee pub in the heart of London. The current building was completed in 1899, during Queen Victoria's reign, but there has been a pub on that site since 1694. The interior is gorgeous, but we chose to sit out in the alleyway where there are a few tables set up, with heaters to make November a nice place to be outside in London. While enjoying said beverage a gentleman approached, asked to share our table, and proceeded to engage us in conversation.

It turned out he was a regular. And his approach and my approach were to ask a lot of questions. We had a rather pleasant 45-minute conversation about the state of politics in America and the UK. And, I honestly think, we were on the opposite side of every issue we discussed. But because we didn't shove our opinions down each other's throats, and simply asked questions, and listened, and challenged, and accepted, and tolerated, and enjoyed, we left as new friends. And we both left with a better understanding of politics from the perspective of someone who was completely different from ourselves.

I think the world needs more of this. Every day. I long for the day when we can once again discuss politics without relationships being destroyed and walls being built. But until that day, a "safe" way to discuss politics (or at least as close to safe as you can come) is to ask questions, listen, and decide to accept the other opinions as a valid expression of belief, even if you don't agree with them at all. I think it makes us better people when we do that.

But as we wrap up our section on cultural differences and begin to dig into the differences in business practices and professional expectations, we have to return to the genius that is Gervais and end as he ended his piece in Time.

"For the record, I'd rather a waiter say, 'Have a nice day' and not mean it, than ignore me and mean it."

Chapter 3
Business 101

There's a great organization spread across the globe, run by the British Government, called the Department of International Trade or DIT for short. Many of the experts in that group work with British and American companies on a daily basis as these companies invest in and trade with the other country.

US businesses may, at times, have a tendency to think a bit bigger from the word go. "US companies are aiming for a certain scale and rate of growth, whereas British businesses can be a bit more measured in their approach," a senior member of Her Majesty's Government told me recently. "There are pros and cons to both approaches, of course."

I can certainly concur with him. In my experience, UK companies also seem to have less appetite for risk as well as underestimating how much planning is needed to make a good entry into the US market. There is also a lack of understanding, many times, about the US federal system and how doing business in Missouri for example is far different from doing business in New York. In fact, British companies should look at each US state as a separate territory and approach each one with a specific plan to operate within that state's cultural and business environment.

New York is more of a snappy, straight-down-to-business type environment, whereas Missouri is more relational, and more vested in the success of companies that choose to invest there. Missouri would be the place for coffee or tea to get to know each other first, or even a meal. You will actually find this working well in many places outside of New York.

Marketing materials are also a matter of difference. British companies who are experienced with working in the US have some phenomenal marketing materials, some of which I have gleaned inspiration from over the years. However, British companies who are venturing into the US for the first time are, more commonly, lacking in marketing materials, and even a marketing strategy. I highly recommend you engage with a US-based marketing agency who understands your target audience in order to produce materials that capture the essence of your company, in a British way, but at a level of production expected in the US. And don't feel that has to be a New York or Los Angeles agency. You can find some amazing firms all across America, including in my current home town of St. Louis, Missouri, at a much lower price point.

Another thing for British companies to be aware of, is that no matter how big and successful your product or brand is in the UK, there's a good chance no one has heard of it in the US. Don't make the dangerous assumption that they already know you. It's better to plan to build your reputation from zero, and then find out they already knew you, than to assume they know you and then be unable to generate awareness.

The final point of advice for British companies is to not get bogged down on the granular details of your company and your product. British companies have a tendency to spend the first 15-30 minutes going through the 300 years of company history before getting to the substance of the conversation. For Americans, a five-minute overview is fine, and then move to the substance. Most American companies will be impressed with something like, "we've been in business since 1486, making the best saddles for the traveler of the day. Today, we are creating the latest innovations that every traveler now and in the future will need."

We'll dig into all this a little deeper as we move through this book. But now let's chat about American companies doing business in the UK.

My friend at SDI shared his perspective that UK companies are much more risk averse than their American counterparts. "UK businesses tend to be more apologetic in tone," he told me, "whereas American businesses are focused on selling their brand in a direct manner."

You may have heard at times an American talking about failing fast, and you may wonder why people in the US who have had multiple business failures continue to find funding and backers for their business ventures.

It comes down to a simple mindset. Americans in business value the lessons learned by making mistakes or failing in a business. The key to going at it again is to learn from what happened, improving your next product or company, and having more success next time. This, historically, has not been a mindset in the UK. Now, not all Americans are like this, but many are.

You do hear this same language in the UK. I was recently in Cambridge, meeting with some incredibly sharp and innovative organizations in the agtech or agritech sector. And during one conversation about investing in companies, which they are doing a great job of in that area of the UK, the term "quick to fail" was used in a positive sense. This was the first time I had ever heard this from a British investor, and this particular speaker received a very positive response from the 15 Americans who were listening. It seems that this mindset may be establishing itself in the UK, but don't make that assumption quite yet as one example does not make a trend. But I hope it does.

There is still, as a whole, a significant difference in business mindset. Process is different. Outcomes are different. Deliverables are different. Although, to digress, I have noticed that lean processes do seem to be a great combination of British process with US outcomes.

But back to the differences in doing business in the UK as an American business.

American business is more direct. British business is more subtle, less direct, more self-deprecating. Brits will ever so nicely tell you they are not interested in doing business, but it usually takes a while for the American company that's new to all this to figure out that it's just been told to move along. They are also more proper, unless a late-night drinking bout is the venue. And it will take quite a while for Brits to open up about personal matters, if they ever do.

Americans should tone down their bragging, even if they can back everything up. The stereotypical American is viewed as a loud, obnoxious braggard with no tact and with expectations that everyone is there to serve them. Any Brit who really knows Americans knows that this is absolutely not true, but please, please, do your best not to add to this awful stereotype.

One key sector that warrants some significant foreknowledge is the defense industry. A good friend of mine here in Missouri, Jim Hager, CEO of Arnold Defense, has significant experience doing business with the British defense sector.

"Generally speaking, the British Ministry of Defence is much tighter lipped and security conscious than we, in America, tend to be," he told me recently. "This can often lead to frustration and the belief that nothing is happening because they have exhaustive vetting procedures that typically slow the process to a crawl. That said, once the Brits have completed their investigation, they are an amicable and loyal partner."

In Jim's opinion, Britain sees the US as a major marketing conglomeration that will say whatever is necessary to make a sale. This then requires an American business to prove their claims more than they would need to do when selling in the US. Not a bad thing to be able to do, but something to keep top of mind.

Other challenges according to Jim include time differences, product delivery and customs issues, contract law differences, product support and information exchange limitations.

"Finally, as is the case almost everywhere, there is a strong 'not invented here' or 'we can do that better' mentality that must be dealt with and overcome," Jim said.

"Oftentimes this leads to product improvement, but sometimes it's just an obstacle to be overcome."

But it is overcome-able. As Jim's success globally with Arnold Defense can attest to.

The other items that are different, and there are many, are views of investment (Brits lean more towards public funding, whereas Americans lean towards private), regulatory expectations, legal process, social norms, how you pitch, and the view of government's role in things. Ok, so pretty much everything.

But there are enough commonalities to start from, and with some hard work, some passion for building a deal, and a little luck, you can build a vibrant cross-Atlantic business arrangement that benefits everyone involved.

Chapter 4
Business Etiquette and Small Talk

As we have already established, American and British ways of communicating and doing business are different. Business people, and especially lawyers, in the UK like to abide by a process and are quite methodical and intentional in terms of next steps. You will find the need for a lot of communication back and forth on the process and until there is an agreement on process, an American company should not expect to move forward to the substance of any particular deal.

Going the other way, British companies should not take the American desire to get working on the deal the wrong way. There is a high level of optimism and building something together from the American perspective. America has always been the land of dreams, and the sky is the limit for a lot of businesses. The reality is always somewhere between the aspirations and the worst-case scenario, but the optimism and vision of American companies can be somewhat disconcerting to British business people.

Things to keep in mind as you enter this initial phase of relationship building, because that's really what it is, is that both of you, regardless of which country you are from, are most likely doing something you've never done before, or you wouldn't be reading this book. You are walking into a process you've never done, with a culture you have probably made inaccurate assumptions about, in a deal that could make or break your career. No pressure.

So, big questions need to be answered. What to expect, how to manage different perspectives, and what the heck the other culture actually means by the words they use. Communication and a trusting relationship are key to your success. And that takes time to build.

Some advice once given to me by an American lawyer who works a lot of UK-US deals on behalf of a successful British business leader is that he always tries to take a deferential approach, and actively works to avoid any perception as the "ugly American" who wants to "dictate" how things should unfold. He recommends asking a lot of questions of the British company representatives, such as "How do you see this unfolding?" or "How do you see this progressing?" with a goal of at least starting a substantive conversation that can move things forward.

This deferential and polite approach helps establish him as someone who respects and can be respected in return.

And this isn't just for Americans dealing with Brits. Deference and politeness work both ways. Ultimately, you are trying to develop a cooperative process where both parties are working to the same ends, using an agreed process that all parties are comfortable with.

And these relationships are entirely possible and should be pursued. This same American lawyer had nothing but positive things to say about the Brits he had worked with over the years. His experiences have been entirely positive, solidly healthy, and have enabled him to develop many strong relationships with British lawyers and accountants.

So, what about small talk? The name seems to indicate something that really is a waste and just something you do to pass the time. But I contend that it is an essential part of the beginning of the relationship.

Try this.

You are an American company in London or Edinburgh for the first time, meeting with your potential business partners, or you are in New York or St. Louis as a British company. Go out to dinner and drinks and get to know each other. Yes, Americans tend to be more open and direct in these situations, and Brits more reserved. But it is a great foundation to build. Yes, Americans are more impatient than their British counterparts, but a chat over a pint is a great thing to do. Now, it's not as bad as doing business with the Italians (no offense as I love Italy and one of my best mates is an Italian in Australia) but dealing with the Italians can take days, weeks and months to work through things, mostly I think due to the actual work day starting around four in the afternoon, even though your day with them started at nine in the morning.

Now the Brits do not have that kind of pace, but they are certainly not as aggressive and impatient as the Americans. But what is similar is the need to build that relationship and that trust. Americans need to avoid being a wee bit cowboy.

In Britain, the swaggering cowboy who makes his own way in the world and builds his own success, alone, is, well, perceived as arrogant. Americans must be sensitive to this, and Brits need to realize that Americans, for the most part, are not arrogant, just confident.

Americans should also avoid putting UK companies on the spot. These are big decisions, with big money and careers on the line. Allow companies and individuals the time to reflect and decide on next steps they are comfortable with. Trying to push a British company into a decision will not work well. The reaction may be polite, but from that point on the Brits are looking for the best way to exit.

Stepping back briefly to the going out for dinner and drinks, there is a significant cultural difference between how American business people and British business people approach this. Now, I spend most of my time in America, so I am much more familiar with the American cultural scene. And it always seems to catch me off guard, just a little, with how much Brits are comfortable drinking in a business setting. Some would claim that Brits can handle their drinks better, and I would probably agree with that. But I have lost count of the times, in a business or governmental setting, where it has become obvious that various individuals are completely soused and will probably not remember most of the conversation we are having when they crawl out of bed in the morning.

So, Americans, be aware of this, almost expect it, and then it won't mess up a good business deal. Brits, slow down a wee bit and be aware that heavy drinking in a business environment, no matter which side of the Pond you are on, can cause a negative reaction in the Americans you are dealing with.

As CEO of StrathKirn Inc and fellow GlobalScot Jim McLaren told me, this is all about trust and you can tell pretty quickly if these two companies are going to get along and build that trust by just that first meeting whether over dinner, over drinks or just in an office setting.

Chapter 5

I Didn't Mean to Give that Impression

One key element both countries must keep at the top of their minds is the fact that difference in perspective and culture can cause interactions and conversations to be interpreted differently than intended.

"British companies should not be too modest," was the response from a senior member of the British Government when I brought this issue up to him. "British companies should tell Americans what they are good at, and why they should invest in or buy from them." The sad truth is, many business deals have not happened because the British way of understating their expertise has been interpreted by American companies as meaning the Brits can't do what the Americans thought they could.

I've seen it in the startup scene in particular. If you pitch in the US, like you would pitch in the UK, you won't be taken seriously as they will see you as lacking confidence in your product. If you pitch in the UK like you would pitch in the US, you will come across as arrogant and braggadocios and, as a result, not someone to be taken seriously. The key to circumventing this issue is to acknowledge the differences in pitching from the beginning, so expectations are set, and cultural differences are minimized.

To build on that, US companies should not think that irony or self-deprecation means that a UK company or individual is not world class. In fact, the more self-deprecating someone is, it may just mean that they are one of the more successful individuals you've come across.

In fact Brits, you need to almost oversell yourselves when dealing with American companies. Not really, but it will probably feel like that as you are not used to that approach. At the very least, be confident about your assertions and plans, and make sure that confidence comes across. And don't talk around your plans, actually talk about your plans. Get to the point. Get to the value. And get to the opportunity.

Follow up efforts should also be more assertive than you are used to when you, a Brit, are dealing with an American. The follow up phase is an important phase in America, and Brits, you have a tendency to not take this phase in your business dealings as seriously and as importantly as you should.

A Resume or curriculum vitae (CV) is the same way. They are not written the same way in both countries, although they are similar.

Resumes in the U.S. are normally one page in length, although two pages are not uncommon, and include contact information, a professional summary, key relevant past employment usually targeted where you are applying, awards information, volunteer service and key skills you hold.

CVs in the UK are often longer and include more details. You should include all relevant work history, in reverse chronological order, and don't feel limited by the one to two-page limit normal in the US. You also don't need to limit your work experience to the last 10 or so years. If there is relevant experience further back in your career, include it. You might also include an interests and achievements section, that expands on an awards or recognition section you might find in a U.S. resume. However, this is not the place for you to position yourself as a needlepoint expert or karaoke guru (unless that's the job you're going for). Make sure the interests are somewhat relevant to the job.

Keep it concise and clear and use bullets if possible. Use active verbs and avoid generic phraseology.

Finally, for a UK CV, make sure you are spelling everything the correct way. Um, I mean, the British way. And have someone else proof read it. Also, specific references are not necessary for either a resume or a CV, those will be requested later. The statement "references available upon request" needed is not needed either, because, well, you would hope so.

And for both a resume and a CV, include a cover letter that personalizes your credentials, and helps explain any gaps or targets in experience for the role you are applying for.

Additionally, as a US visitor to the British business scene, don't just visit London or the southeast of England. There is so much more. I recently assisted in leading an agtech business delegation from the US to the UK, and we made sure to include visits to York and Cambridge, and also include organizations from Scotland, Wales and Northern Ireland. Future visits with this group will include on-the-ground visits to Scotland, Wales and Northern Ireland.

Politics is a dangerous area to engage in, as people do tend to get defensive on both sides of the Pond when outsiders criticize. I mentioned this already, but it is important to stress. My overall guidance is 'listen to learn,' without giving your opinion about the other country's way of doing things.

Other things to watch out for that could leave a bad impression are things like tipping. This is especially true for Brits in the US. In much of the US, tips are part of an expected income for servers, and the norm is right around a 20 percent tip. And for Yanks, while a tip is not expected in the UK, it is appreciated. But don't feel like you have to tip.

Staying on the subject of food, don't complain about local cuisine. Globally, there is pride in the food each community is known for. In Missouri, try the barbecue, enjoy the toasted ravioli, and indulge in the gooey butter cake. And if you don't like it, keep your mouth shut. In the

UK, haggis is safe (it's basically lamb sausage), spotted dick is actually a delicious dessert (and a favorite of my good friend Mark Reardon of KMOX Radio fame in St. Louis, Missouri), and the variety and quality of food available will astound anyone who is not a regular visitor. One of these days I hope to take weeks and just eat my way through the United Kingdom. In London alone, I could have a different ethnic cuisine every day and it would take months to run out of choices.

Also, visitors to the UK should be conscious of speaking too loudly. Growing up in the UK, my opinion of Americans was the loud, brightly dressed, overweight tourists with cameras and bad manners. This is absolutely not true, but don't cause people to think of you as the "ugly American" by the way you act.

Overall, just be careful with espousing your opinions in anything but a positive way. No one likes the opinionated person from, well, anywhere, who comes to town and disparages the place where you live and work. Find the positives, focus on those, and leave any negatives unsaid.

According to Chris Jamroz, a private equity executive educated in the UK and the US, there are little differences in how you approach investors in London versus New York if you are a mature company. The big difference where people from the UK struggle is an assumption that investors or companies in the US have the same global outlook that people in Europe have. And this mindset difference sometimes makes the difference between connecting with your partners or investors, and not.

By virtue of location, even the type of news you will see on the evening newscast is vastly different in London than in the US. People in the US do not see as much global news, especially if it does not have an immediate and apparent impact on US day-to-day interests. And this difference in perception can have a significant impact on how you introduce yourself in business.

For example, if you as a UK company are introducing yourself as a global company with a solid growth strategy in Africa or Australia, you will not be as interesting to many US partners than if you had a US-centric growth strategy or value proposition. You might actually find one of your less-than-stellar competitors, who you know has less to offer potential US partners, as being perceived as more attractive due to their positioning to a US market.

To boil it down, "focus on the benefit in America, for American companies, and never be afraid to state the obvious," Chris said. "Don't assume that American companies or Americans know things that a European might know." And vice versa.

Americans are fairly risk averse when using overseas vendors or putting their trust in someone who is not already in the US. This can be incredibly frustrating but the firms who are successful do not get bothered by this. They instead find their way around this reality.

Another observation that Chris has made over the years is that Americans expect to get almost everything accomplished in the first meeting. They expect decisions to be made based on imperfect data sets and are not as interested in process. They are interested in outcome and how to make things happen.

And Americans are very comfortable with people within a team taking very visible leadership roles within a project and being unapologetically confident in their success. In the UK, this would have the danger of being perceived as arrogant. What UK companies need to remember in this situation is that Americans are still committed to teamwork but are terrified of "decision making by committee."

Americans, especially when they are first working with a UK company, are going to be looking for a single decision maker that they can work with and through in order to make things efficient and expedient. Chris calls it the "velocity of decision making." It describes a key difference in mindset between investing time to evaluate and consider and debate and intellectually challenge and get it perfect on the UK side of the Pond in order to reach the right decision, and the US perspective of having an expedient decision-making process to get to a decision quickly and then adjust in real time going forward.

Chris's advice for Brits is to be clear, to the point, and "rude," as this will be perceived in the US as effective, efficient and clear. This approach gets people comfortable, engaged, and moving forward.

Chapter 6
Code Words

We started off with some funny examples of words that have different meanings in the other country, and not understanding them could result in some rather funny stories or stressful situations. However, this is also true for business dealings.

Each type of business within a country has its own set of terms that are used, so imagine how complicated it might be when working internationally. Let's say, you are an American and in your first meeting with a UK counterpart who wants to learn more about your business, they ask, "What's your remit, and what turnover are you seeing?" You pause, and strongly consider asking the English lad to speak, well, English.

Allow me to bail you out. Remit basically means your tasking or focus as a company, or what your stakeholders expect you to do. Turnover is the British term for revenue, not, as you might have thought, loss of employees. Other words that you might run across might be a little easier to understand would be things like annual leave, meaning vacation time. But don't assume anything. Repeat back items that you may not be clear on and try to avoid trying to look good when you really have no idea what the other person was talking about. Remember, this is a business relationship you are cultivating, and in order for it to succeed, and for you to have a clear understanding of next steps and what success might look like, the communication has to be incredibly clear and concise.

Within the venture capital (VC) areas, you will find a lot of shared vernacular, but you will occasionally run across words that mean different things, like the aforementioned turnover. Also in the VC area, perspectives on deal sizes are different, with Brits focused on smaller deals as a whole. However, that's not always true. I have a great friend in a large British company who won't even start thinking about a deal below $15 million, with a tendency to be closer to $50 million or more.

And then there's the word "quite."

There's the common meaning, that is used in both countries, meaning "completely." For example, "You are quite correct." It has the same meaning regardless of what side of the Pond you are on.

However, what about "quite good?" In the UK, "quite good" means "pretty good" or "fairly good." But in the US, it tends to mean "very good" or "really good."

Some other words you may run across as a Yank in the UK could include:

- Barmy, meaning crazy or unbalanced
- Barrister or advocate, which are specific types of lawyers in England or Scotland
- The Beeb, otherwise known as the BBC
- Biro, a ballpoint pen
- Blower, the telephone (not to be confused with a telly which is a TV)
- Bodge, which is basically a cheap or poor performance or job
- Building society, which is an institution owned by depositors rather than shareholders
- Bunce, a windfall or profit

And that's just a handful of the B words.

Bottom line, there's a whole lot of words you can find in the UK that most Yanks would have no clue about, and vice versa. Check out Appendix B at the end of the book for a more complete list of these "code words."

Chapter 7

Making the Pitch

Let's be direct (a very un-British thing for me to do).

If an American comes to Britain to pitch their new startup and ask for funding and partnership in the way that is normal in the US, that person will be viewed as arrogant and a braggard and will not be believed. If a Brit pitches in the US like they do in the UK, they will be perceived as lacking confidence and not believing in their product. This is a cultural issue that can kill your dreams upon landing.

Some things to remember when pitching are simple directness and clarity. I think the Yanks need to work on clarity, and the Brits need to work on directness. But both principles apply to both countries.

Oh, and practice. You need to practice your pitch. And then practice it some more. And then, when you think it's perfect, practice it a few more times. Make sure it is direct and concise. And short. For crying out loud, keep it short. Pick someone to give the pitch who is a good speaker, who can deliver good information, and who can do it efficiently, relatably, and professionally. Leave the technical experts for the follow up questions after the pitch, or later in the process.

A friend of mine who works for the Scottish Government puts it this way. "US pitching is more direct, concise, and focused, whereas UK pitching tends to offer more information and take a bit longer," he says. "American companies may want to provide more information than they're used to when delivering sales pitches, but maintain their focus on their unique selling proposition, while UK companies would do well to shorten their presentations and really focus on delivering a clear sales message when in the US."

"First impressions are very important," according to John Loudon, President of the Gonzalez Family Office in Palm Beach, Florida. John, a regular talking head on national television, receives pitches from companies looking for funding on a regular basis.

"You need to be able to support your track record and make the case you have a unique value-add," he continues. "We want to know 'what are you disrupting?' And expect us to be skeptical, so be ready for the hard follow-up questions. You need to know what things could trip up your business, what your return to investors will be and what your timeline is—at a bare minimum."

John also stressed the importance of tax efficiencies, the ability for investors to collect on tax credits, and getting other known investors involved.

"If Warren Buffet is involved for example, then other investors will follow."

John's firm also crunches a lot of data when evaluating companies, so you need to have every bit of information available when they do their due diligence. You need the track record of success on the team, both in the current project and in past projects, and it is essential that you are up to speed on the current regulatory environment and the latest available incentives and credits.

"If a company walks in and understands Opportunity Zones, and includes that in their pitch, we are going to pay attention," John said.

He also recommends attending investor conferences and leveraging the "speed dating" they offer there. These could be general investor conferences such as Invest Midwest, or more focused national conferences such as Finovate.

Chapter 8
Closing the Deal

We've talked previously about the need to build relationships across the Pond in order for your business dealings to be successful. Both parties, as in any business dealings, need to agree on success and process. But that doesn't mean a handshake with a trusted business associate is all you need. Especially when you are dealing with intellectual property.

Once you get close to closing the deal, that's when the paperwork becomes really, really … really important. This protects you, them, and the process because you have something concrete to reference at all times.

For example, if you have a huge amount of intellectual property, or even just a small amount, it is absolutely essential you figure out licensing and ownership in clearly written form in order to protect everyone's interests going forward.

Many times, contracts dealing with patents and trademarks and support coming from the UK are more simplistic than in the US. American companies are much more used to complexity than UK companies, although in Britain's defense that has been changing in recent years. The UK legal system today seems to be approaching contracts, any type of contract such as supply agreements or licensing, in a more similar way to how things have been handled in the US system. Culturally, this may be a difficult obstacle to overcome as having a contract come back from a US company with enough red ink and corrections to make your favorite school teacher blush could cause the "ugly American" reaction to occur in the minds of the Brits involved. What you need to remember is that this is the product of a legal environment that requires specificity and clarity, rather than the looser system British companies are used to.

Which is an interesting paradox. On the one hand, us Brits are precise in so many things, such as process, but then when the final contract comes along that precision seems to ebb due to the legal environment Brits are used to operating in. And if we Brits are going to take comeuppance at anything, it's being accused of a lack of precision. Brits are all about precision and take pride in that.

But when it comes to contracts, Americans have much more detailed contract expectations as a general rule. Now, this is changing, but this historical perspective is important to have especially if you are engaging in business across the Pond for the first time. It is likely that the Brit will find the American challenging them to be a wee bit more precise.

Key questions to be asking yourself at this point is what am I walking into, what do I need to watch out for, who do I need in the room to make sure this gets wrapped up right for the long term? Do I need local council in both countries who understand international law? Do I need a "translator" who speaks both business languages? What about social laws? What about employment related laws? What about finance law, or just banking perspectives? Actually, having a local investment banker or a middleman at this point, and throughout, can be a rather wise idea in order to navigate all the nuances involved. An international tax expert is also incredibly useful to have on hand.

It's also helpful that the "middleman" be someone who is trusted by both parties. This is, ultimately, all about relationships and an ongoing working situation, and having a trusted middleman, especially for that first deal between companies, who speaks both "languages" can be a life saver.

Additionally, repetition is not a bad thing. And what I mean by that is repeating what you heard back to the other person. We know that things are said that to one person might not mean much, but to the other person might be a deal clincher, or a deal killer, if they move forward with that item top of mind. You should be quick to say, "If I'm hearing you right, then ..." and then repeat back what you heard. This allows for clarity and complete transparency. And you can't be afraid to do that. You know the cultures are different now, and you need to do everything you can to make sure you are all on the same page, understanding what is being said in the same way, so the path towards a deal is clear, and the path beyond the deal is clear.

You must work to ensure that all gaps are filled, or at least bridged.

Let's get specific. British companies don't like to tell you they are not interested. Repeating back, transparency, and clear understanding allows you to figure out if there is actually a deal here. You can't be afraid to gently press a point in order to make sure you are getting all the information.

And Americans, don't be surprised that the outcome of a meeting is a list of targets. Also, don't be surprised that if those targets are not met then the Brits will have an updated list of targets to meet. Brits are all about process.

Brits, Americans are not used to that. They are used to goals, and they are going to figure out how to hit that goal within the timeline agreed to.

Very different approaches. And if you don't understand this about each other, you can end up parting on bad terms with no success.

But you also need to roll with the punches and decide whether you can live with the difference, or if you need to counter something that it becomes clear you are not on the same page about. If something is pretty flagrantly off the charts, then yes, spend some time on that item and see if you can come to an agreement. But if it is a small issue, then deference and tolerance can go a long way in building the relationship. Try to be deferential and respectful of a position and try to work within the parameters desired.

Americans, you now have a list of targets, that may or may not be met. But remember, at least you have a process to work through with your new British friends. And a process, even if not what you are used to, is a good thing to have. A common ground to work from. Everyone has a common understanding of what lies ahead, and that, any day of the week, is a good place to be in a business relationship.

Chapter 9

Socializing and Work/Life Balance

It has been said that the pub is the real British parliament, where debates take place, drinks are held high, and people become friends over a pint. And it is absolutely true.

As I mentioned earlier, during a recent visit to London, I found myself sitting outside a pub in Covent Garden, chatting with one of the regulars—a rare Londoner born in London. We were far apart on everything political, with two very different backgrounds, yet we chatted for more than an hour on all things British and American, including politics, religion and bad jokes. We could not have been further apart in mindset, yet we parted friends. We both challenged each other a little, and we both were challenged a little.

This is not abnormal in London, and even more common outside of London. The pub is the center of society in many places, and it's where the vicar, the mayor, the local drunk, and every other walk of life raise a glass together on a regular basis.

It is however, unfortunately, abnormal in the USA. Today, for a Brit, be careful what topics you bring up as you may be surprised where the American you are getting to know stands. For example, there are successful business people who are strong supporters of President Trump. There are others who are opposed to everything he stands for. If you are curious, you can ask. But don't be surprised with the strength of the position that comes back your way, as both sides of the political spectrum are rather polarized these days. And also, it's always better to ask questions, rather than giving your opinion. "I've heard" is a much better way to keep things friendly than "I think."

Also, if you are out for a pint, don't forget to tip in the US, and don't expect to tip in the UK. In the UK, tipping is not part of the culture, whereas it is in the US. Twenty percent is a good amount in the US, or a dollar a drink if that makes it easier. But, if you've had a good time chatting with the British bartender, a couple of quid left on the bar is never not appreciated.

One thing to watch out for Brits in America, and that's how much you drink. At a networking event in the US for example, where alcohol is served, 1-3 drinks is normal. No one gets sloshed, and everyone usually avoids being the topic of conversation the next day. I've noticed, many times, that when Brits hang out in America at the bar, they drink to the point of inebriation. While what you do on your own time is your own business, if business is involved it does not leave a good impression.

Also, Yanks in the UK, don't try to keep up. You are most likely a lightweight, and even if the Brits behave themselves and stay relatively sober, there's a good chance if you are matching them drink-for-drink, that you may be a little ... not sober.

Another point to think about is lunch. In the UK a pint at lunch is pretty normal. In the US, very rare. Easiest way to gauge, follow the lead of your hosts. And also remember that you may be a little jetlagged when you first arrive so be careful with that alcohol if you do indulge.

Just like socializing and work/life balance are different between LA and New York, and somewhere like Missouri, there are also significant differences between the UK and the US. And, just like the regional differences in the US, there are also those in the UK. And of course, age makes a difference everywhere as well.

If you look at the US, you've got cities built around their music scenes, micro-breweries and getting outdoors. Austin, Denver, Nashville, and Kansas City would all fall into this category. Major sports cities such as St. Louis have a lot of focus on their baseball, ice hockey, basketball and more. Yes, I know I'm over simplifying, as St. Louis also has amazing Blues music, fun micro-breweries, and brilliant wineries in the hills outside the city. But the key point is that different cities and regions of the country do things differently.

New York is very different, with a heavy focus on theatre, events and a 24/7 style of living.

You'll find that same difference when you compare London with York or Edinburgh, or Cardiff. London is a large, international city with flavors of life of all sorts, packed with tourists, heavy in history. York is more relaxed, with history everywhere, good pubs, and a slower pace of life. Cambridge is even more relaxed, as it is an innovative college town with startups and breathtaking architecture. Edinburgh is a welcoming city, with great street festivals and open-air events, combined with history and historic shopping districts, and coffee shops and the smallest bar in the UK.

In the actual socializing, you'll probably find that Americans watch and talk about TV more, although Netflix is changing that divide as we all watch similar programs these days.

Also, religion plays a bigger part in the lives of many Americans, and they are more comfortable talking about it. For many people, what they do in business is impacted by their religion, and how they operate in business is certainly impacted by religion for those who adhere to it more strongly.

Politics as well, although I have noticed a shift in the past ten years or so that has more Brits talking openly about politics. But, don't make assumptions. This is an issue just within major cities in America, so imagine trying to guess the political persuasion of someone from another country. You, as a Brit, may meet a successful American entrepreneur and assume he's liberal as you would define a liberal. However, he may be, and probably is, an interesting mix of things. He could be involved in healthcare, and be frustrated with government regulations, therefore leaning him more conservative. But he could also have a passion for serving those who lack medical care, which means he could be more liberal. But his passion for serving others could be based in his religion, so he could be more conservative. You get my drift. Don't make assumptions. Find common ground and be ready to learn and accept.

Brits, here's a bonus, from a friend in the UK Government at the UK Embassy in Washington DC. Americans, generally, love the Royal Family. And are thrilled if you've ever even seen one of them. Use that to generate fun conversations. It's a favorite topic of mine because I hold The Queen in such high regard. But even if you don't, Americans are fascinated by it and are shocked to find out just how much power she really does have, as the Prime Minister of Australia found out the hard way a few years back.

I mentioned sports earlier, and that's also not a bad thing for everyone to learn more about. Brits, watch the Super Bowl, learn about baseball, and try to figure out basketball.

Basketball is certainly a challenge for me. Two of my kids have played and I spent the first year rather confused as to what the heck was going on with all the whistles and penalties. But you can get there, and Americans love to talk about their sports teams, and are convinced they would do a better job than the coach.

The same is true for Americans. Learn about British football. You know, the sport where you actually use your foot to move a ball around and don't have to take a break every couple of yards. Or rugby, which is a fascinating sport that I'm just now starting to get into. Watch the Premier League, pick a team, and engage with the Brits in conversation.

Some other items related to socializing, would be how you order drinks and food in bars. In America, you are used to finding a table, sitting down, and a waitress comes over to take your orders and brings them to your table. That's uncommon in the UK. The more likely scenario is that you order everything at the bar, pay, grab your drinks and they will bring your food to you when it's ready. Also, you will pay every time you order a drink or a round. There is also no expectation for tips in bars, and most restaurants.

In America, when ordering drinks or food, you've got options. Yes, you can still order from the bar, but you also have the table option in many places. You will also most likely run a tab rather than pay every time. This could be done by the bar holding your credit card while you are there, or by simply scanning your card and putting all your orders into the system as the night goes on. Then at the end of the night you settle up. Brits, as mentioned a tiny bit ago, also remember to tip. Twenty percent is normal, less than that can be offensive. And if you have just been ordering a few drinks, usually a $1 per drink for tip is a good measure.

Chapter 10

Insights on Incentives and Investments

Expanding into another country is no small thing. It's a huge deal, with the potential for some devastating mistakes. So, it's incredibly important to have some expert advice from people whose entire job is to help you out.

For American companies looking to invest in the UK, the Department of International Trade (DIT) and Scottish Development International, and the US Commercial Service, can be incredibly helpful. These teams can help you find the right landing place, connect you with funding options, introduce you to similar companies in the UK, and help you understand the vast difference in cost, opportunity and talent across the British Isles.

There are research and development (R&D) tax credits to be aware of, the UK Patent Box which allows companies to apply for a lower rate of corporation tax on profits earned from patented inventions and certain other innovations— currently sitting at a 10 percent rate, and various other local and national benefits, grants and credits.

You can also invest in the UK to get a great foothold into Europe, something that Brexit does not change, and then work with UK Export Finance to access revenue that can help you export from the UK. So long as you have a certain level of British content in what you are selling or researching, they will treat you like you are British.

Aside from the national level sources of funding, there are more regional or local sources. One example I learned about recently was a fund established by the Cambridgeshire and Peterborough Combined Authority (CPCA). They have developed a scheme to invest in the application and commercialization of research and development, new products and processes, supply chain development, and new policies, initiatives and regulations.

The CPCA Growth Fund allows them to cover 25 percent of total project costs in the forms of grants from

£10,000-£150,000. Jobs have to be created or protected as part of the project and the funding has to be used on new or improved products or processes, equipment, energy efficiency, or waste reduction.

In addition to this local Growth Fund, the CPCA has also developed a local R&D Fund that can cover up to 50 percent of the total project costs in grants ranging from £10,000 to £60,000. These grants are focused in on agricultural productivity or food and drink technology and can be used anywhere in the development cycle.

Both these funds are for small businesses, which in this case is defined differently from the standard UK definition of SMEs, as those with less than 250 employees and an annual turnover (profits) of less than 50 million Euros. And the proposed project must take place in the East of England. As of February 2019, the funds have awarded £6 million to 97 projects and have also helped generate an additional £15 million in private sector investment. Jobs created so far total more than 600.

FYI, the traditional definition of an SME or small business in the UK is a company with annual turnover of no more than £6.5 million, a balance sheet of no more than £3.26 million and no more than 50 employees.

Additionally, it's highly possible your state has funds available to help you export, which might be the first step to take before you consider an expansion location in the UK. Missouri's export assistance funds, for example, are run by a team within the Department of Economic Development, and regions around the state also have export assistance funding and programs available to assist you.

For British companies going the other way, the same organizations can help, along with state level or regional groups such as Missouri Partnership or the St. Louis Regional Economic Development Alliance or the Kansas City Area Development Council. Missouri even has a chain of international offices globally, including one in the British Isles, that focus on helping companies interested in entering the US. These organizations exist to make sure you are successful. And, places like St. Louis or Kansas City want you to be successful so you can tell all your mates about them.

Some other examples in Missouri would include the Missouri Technology Corporation, a government run, equity-based funding source for startups, or Arch Grants, a privately-funded non-equity grant that invests $50,000 in companies who expand into Missouri. And of course, there are a plethora of other funding sources at all levels, both grant and traditional equity-based investing. SixThirty in Missouri comes to mind, along with SixThirty Cyber, both investing $100,000 at a time in fintech and cyber companies respectively.

Yield Lab is another option that started in Missouri but has since expanded internationally. They are focused on agtech or agritech investments, usually in the range of $100,000 at a time. They are equity-based, but the beauty of their investment is they want you to stay where you are and be successful. And then every three months or so you travel to St. Louis or one of their other locations for mentoring and other guidance to ensure that their investment is given as much support as possible. And states across America will have similar programs and organizations.

"With the US, my view is that UK firms that do well here in the UK can do amazingly well in the US— transforming their businesses—but there is also perhaps a greater risk here of making some expensive mistakes," a senior British Government official told me. "That's where the Department for International Trade comes in—helping investments in each direction succeed."

There is also a lot of opportunity for research collaborations that cross the Atlantic. I recently helped lead a delegation of Missouri agtech leaders to the UK, and we spent time getting to know the amazing research and development taking place in places like Rothamsted and Cambridge and York, and about the many government-supported centers of excellence across the UK that are looking for American research partners and investors.

"In both countries, we find that there is a strong connection and that you will find lots of people who want to help you," a friend in the UK Embassy in DC told me. "And for investment, both countries are very welcoming."

Chapter 11

A National Zone of Opportunity

As promised, and I am a man of my word, let's talk Opportunity Zones.

To say that I am excited about this new creation here in America would be a severe understatement. I see these Zones as transformative for communities across the US, and an opportunity for any company or organization who has access to funders that have made money in the past.

Allow me to shed some light on the situation.

The Tax Cuts and Jobs Act of 2017, signed by President Trump on December 22, 2017, went into effect on January 1, 2018. This new law did many things, such as lowering the federal corporate tax from 35 percent to 21 percent.

Real quick, as a side note, don't forget there are federal and state taxes to be aware of when looking to invest into the US from the UK.

OK. Back to the Tax Cuts and Jobs Act. Asides from the corporate tax reduction and many other changes, this law established a brand-new type of zone designed to encourage investments in low-income areas across America.

Immediately after this law went into effect, governors from all 50 states went to work. Their task was to propose certain areas of their states to be certified as Federal Opportunity Zones. Each governor then submitted their list of zones to the federal government and the federal government approved them. Missouri, for example, submitted 161 zones across the state. It most likely wasn't that simple, and a whole heck of a lot of work went into this process, but that's the cliffs notes version.

Here's how Opportunity Zones work, with the caveat that I am not a tax attorney or an accountant, simply an entrepreneur who is passionate about investments that create social and economic improvement, and one who has lost count of the number of conversations I have had with developers and investors about Opportunity Zones.

An investor sells a property or a bunch of stocks in the US, and as a result they owe capital gains tax. The purpose of the Opportunity Zones is to encourage that investor to invest those funds in areas of the country he or she may not think about investing in. They are still good areas, but they are areas that have not seen a lot of investment in recent years.

So, the investor … let's call him Donald. So, Donald sold a property and saw a gain of $10 million. He now owes, most likely, a 26 percent tax bill, or $2.6 million. Normally, Donald would roll that gain into the purchase of another building, within 180 days, in order to defer paying that capital gains tax. This is called a 1031 exchange.

Opportunity Zones will trump this process for the time being, and if they become permanent you could see 1031 exchanges becoming a footnote in history.

Under an Opportunity Zone, the 180 days still applies but the structure is different and the opportunity … pun intended … is much greater.

Donald, instead of doing a 1031 exchange and purchasing a building within 180 days, puts his $10 million in an existing Opportunity Fund. Immediately, his capital gains tax is deferred until the end of 2026 (or later if the regulations come out that use years of investment rather than specific dates).

Within the fund the timeline for having to use the money is longer, allowing the Fund to purchase and renovate attractive properties, build from the ground-up, or invest in businesses. The main stipulation at this point on the use of the funds is that 70% of the funds have to be used (or have clear plans to be used) within a Federal Opportunity Zone and that any property you purchase has to have an amount equal to the basis value of the building (just the building value and not the land value) invested in the improvement of the property.

In Donald's case, he uses the $10 million to purchase a 100,000 square foot building in need of a full rehab for $6 million and invests the basis value of the building (just the building not the land it sits on) which we figure at $4 million in value in the rehab for a total investment of $10 million. If this happens, the investment qualifies.

Five years later, the next additional benefit kicks in. If the investment has been in the fund for that entire five years, then 10 percent of the owed capital gains tax (in this case $260,000) is forgiven. Two years later, another 5 percent is forgiven (add $130,000 to the $260,000 for a total tax forgiveness of almost $400,000). Then Donald pays the IRS the remainder of the owed capital gains tax.

Additional caveat. It is currently unclear if the 7-year benefit will still be available after the end of 2019, as the original capital gains tax owed, minus what has been forgiven, becomes due at the end of 2026, which doesn't give you 7 years left to hit your 7-year investment goal if you invest after December 31, 2019.

From this point on, if Donald does everything right, that will be the last capital gains tax check he writes to the IRS.

The next big date is 10 years from the initial investment in the Opportunity Fund. Once that 10-year mark hits, the biggest benefit of Opportunity Zones is realized.

No capital gains taxes owed!

Let me explain.

In year 11, Donald puts up his building for sale. His investment was originally $10 million for the purchase and the rehab. His 100,000 square foot building is now a great business location and is fully leased at $25 per square foot. Using that information, the building is valued at $20 million. Donald finds a large insurance firm who is interested in a leaseback on the building, sells the building to them, and then continues to run the property going forward to create additional income and pay the note to the insurance company.

He has just made $10 million on his building. The original $10 million is already taxes paid, so under normal circumstances he would owe capital gains tax on the additional $10 million, or around $2.3 million, to the IRS.

But he actually now owes no additional taxes to the IRS. Yes, really.

Here's why.

Because the building is in an Opportunity Zone, and because he invested money that was a previous capital gain in an Opportunity Fund that followed the rules set by the law and the regulations, he now gets to reset the basis value of the property to the selling price and pay no taxes on the increase. That $2.3 million that was going to go to the IRS is now Donald's. Tax free.

As I said, this is a massive opportunity for communities across the US, and here in my adopted home state of Missouri. UK companies can find investors who are interested in using Opportunity Zones and as a result get some great landing places here, while delivering added value to their investors due to the increased return after 10 years.

And I think we've only just scratched the surface on the opportunities that we will be able to create within Opportunity Zones. The US government, in the regulations released in April 2019, has clarified the benefits for direct investment in a business that is located in an Opportunity Zone.

If you invest qualified funds in a business located within an Opportunity Zone there are two key requirements to keep in mind. First, at least 90 percent of the investment of the Opportunity Fund must be in a business where substantially all of its tangible assets are in an Opportunity Zone.

Secondly, at least 50 percent of the gross income earned from the business investment must be from the active conduct of business within the Opportunity Zone. This doesn't mean that they are selling to others within the Zone, but in fact, like with a software development company, if a majority of time spent by employees on developing products is when they are at the business location in the Opportunity Zone (or if a majority of revenue earned from that development is from developers in the Opportunity Zone), then the business qualifies. This new regulatory guidance should create not only investment opportunities for existing businesses in a Zone, but also significantly impact where startups choose to locate.

The ten-year holding period still applies for business investment, as do the forgiveness of some owed capital gains in years 5 and 7, but there are now some guidelines that allow the divestiture of investments and then the quick re-investment of those assets in qualified businesses in order to keep the clock moving forward. Once the ten years are up, the Fund can sell its assets and all gains are free from capital gains due to the reset of the basis value.

As my friend Julio Gonzalez, CEO of Engineered Tax Services and who was part of the team that wrote the tax reform legislation, said, "Opportunity Zones have created the necessary stimulus to redevelop areas in need. It will dramatically change the investment landscape for the next decade and open the doors to Urban Development."

Chapter 12
Stop and Drink the London Pride

London has the cultural advantages of being, well, London. In talking with Hadyn Craig, a New Zealand transplant to London, he loves the City, but lives in what Americans would consider the suburbs. But this still allows easy access to the culture and vibrancy of London. The food, I can tell you from personal weight-gain experience, is amazing.

You could plan an entire holiday in London based solely on food. Every variety of ethnic food is available. The Duck and Waffle, on the 40th floor in the heart of The City and open 24/7, is a must visit. In the nearby Shard building, with more amazing views of London, sit a number of restaurants including the Hutong restaurant, serving the best of Northern Chinese dishes.

In other parts of London you can find amazing Indian cuisine at Punjab in Covent Garden, smashing food and wine of all kinds at Christopher's (also in Covent Garden and owned by Lord Paul—a member of the House of Lords, an all-around great guy I have the privilege of knowing, and who recently allowed me to sit on the floor of the House of Lords during a debate, and the author of the foreword of this book), delicious Lebanese at Maison Du Mezze in Leicester Square, fun sushi and burgers at Ichibuns in Chinatown, great Spanish tapas at Pix in Notting Hill and some amazing breakfasts at the nearby Egg Break. And if you are a Churchill fan, make sure you eat at The Clarence, just down the road from 10 Downing Street. It was Sir Winston's favorite watering hole. And then there's the M Restaurant in Victoria with its amazing Argentinian Rump Steak and exclusive house wines that I was privileged to enjoy in the company of the founder of the British Monarchist Society.

If you want traditional London pub food and a selection of London brews, then head for, well … the pub. I recommend The Salisbury and The Lamb and Flag, two of the oldest pubs in Covent Garden, with The Lamb and Flag being four years older than the USA and the favorite watering hole of Charles Dickens.

London is full of culture, some thousands of years old. The British Museum welcomes you, for free, with the Rosetta Stone. Ramses II, Assyrian statues, Greek sculptures, and much more are everywhere you turn. It is breathtaking to stand in the midst of world history, and to reach out and touch it. And there are many other museums and galleries to choose from.

If British history is more your cup of tea, then head to Westminster Abbey and the new Queens Gallery. So much history took place, and is buried, in Westminster Abbey. And the new Queens Gallery has items from throughout the history of the British monarchy and allows you a stunning view of where the future King and Queen, The Duke and Duchess of Cambridge walked down the aisle.

Nearby, you can see the famous black door of 10 Downing Street. While you can't actually get into 10 Downing Street or even onto Downing Street, you can take a quick look from the Whitehall front gates and see the street, step and famous black door with the iconic number 10 on it. The police on duty are usually friendly and willing to answer questions (and maybe even take a photo with you), but if they tell you to do something, just do it. They have their reasons, and they're usually good ones.

Once you've stared down the street for a while, take a walk. Back up towards Parliament is the blue door to the Scotland Office, and all around you are buildings you will recognize from many movies, especially the rooftop shots from James Bond's Skyfall.

Done with Whitehall and the Prime Minister? Not quite? Well, since you are in the area already, head on over to my favorite museum in all of London (due to the fact that Sir Winston is, and always will be, my hero), the Churchill War Rooms.

This (no-longer) secret World War II bunker and museum tells the story of Winston Churchill's life and legacy. Once inside you can see where Sir Winston spent much of the war planning and fighting against the Axis forces. And leading the Allies to victory!

What makes it even more impactful is that the Map Room has remained exactly as it was left on the day the lights were switched off in 1945. They basically walked out and locked the doors at the end of the war, and it sat undisturbed until the rooms were re-discovered decades later.

The London Eye is also across the Thames, and a tour of the Houses of Parliament is not to be missed. This is something to do at least twice. Once for the guided tour and once to sit in one of the galleries and watch parliamentary democracy in action.

The guided tour will get you into places a self-guided tour will not, plus you will learn all sorts of fascinating things and possibly get playfully harassed by the tour guide should they discover you are Scottish or American. The history of the place is amazing, and the sights are beautiful.

Once you're done with the guided element, head back to the entry gate to gain access to the House Gallery. The best time to visit is during Prime Minister's Question Time on Wednesdays at noon. But even if you can't get in then, it's well worth the visit. But remember, no hats allowed.

After a day of museums, history and culture, you may need to cut loose and head over to Bunga Bunga in Battersea, for Thursday night karaoke. This was a favorite hangout of the younger royals in days past.

Buckingham Palace is another must visit while in London, and every other day the Changing of the Guard takes place at 11am. And, if you are there in Autumn, there's a chance the Palace will be open for tours or one of the exclusive private tours sometimes available from Christmas until early February. I have been privileged to take a private tour of the Palace, and I am of the opinion that it would be worth flying into the UK just to take the tour. It is breathtaking and inspirational.

Speaking of Her Majesty, just a Tube and train ride away is her home on most weekends—Windsor Castle. Take the audio tour and learn about the history of a castle that has been the home of the British monarch for more than 1,000 years. At the end of the guided tour, you will find yourself standing next to Her Majesty's private courtyard. When I was there recently, a small group of people happened to be showing out some Austrian guests on the far side of the courtyard at what I discovered was the Queen's private entrance. One was a tall gentleman in a military uniform, the other a shorter lady in a lovely blue dress. As I stood there, wondering who was important enough to be showing out guests at Windsor Castle, the realization hit me. It was in fact, Her Majesty. Now, I don't promise you will time it to where you will see our Monarch in person, but you might.

After visiting with Her Majesty, don't forget to do a little shopping around the Castle and grab a bite to eat in the Drury House Restaurant, serving since the 1700s and somewhat reminiscent of Harry Potter-esque stylings. And engage in conversation while there. The last time I was there my wife and I started chatting with the gentleman at the next table, only to discover he worked at Windsor Castle, taking care of Her Majesty's horses. And he had some fun stories to share with us.

For shopping elsewhere, don't miss Harrods, or Saturday's Portobello Market in Notting Hill, or Oxford Street, or Covent Garden, or … well … there are stores everywhere.

Then take a walk through the gardens at Kensington Palace or across Hyde Park or St. James' Park. Kensington Palace is much more than just gardens. First, just walking up to the gates takes your breath away. The grounds and the building are beautiful, and the limited view of the private cottages just make you want to stand there for a chance at a glimpse of royalty. Once you get inside, the visit gets even better. Amazing historic paintings, insights into the life of Queen Victoria or Princess Diana, seeing how King George II and his wife Queen Caroline lived while in the Palace, or just wandering up the King's Staircase. It all brings history to life in a memorable way.

And if you want more history, then spend some time in the Tower of London. A prison, a fortress and a palace—all rolled into one. The Tower of London is a must visit. I highly recommend the guided tour, as your tour guide will be a Yeoman Warder with a sadistic skill for morbid story telling. Once the tour is completed, take a passing glance at the crown jewels. Nothing to see there. Just 23,578 gemstones that are still used in royal ceremonies today embedded in history, culture and ceremony. And then keep moving to see armory, cannons, cells, rooms, sites of beheadings and splendor.

There is enough to do at the Tower to spend an entire day there. And if you do, then you might get to be part of the Ceremony of the Keys, which happens every night—for at least 700 years. But whatever you do, don't take the ravens with you when you leave. Britain will never forgive you if you do.

If you enjoy sports and are lucky enough to be in London during Wimbledon, don't miss the chance to experience this world-class event, even if you can only get on the grounds (which is a challenge in itself). Unless you know someone with Sir or Lord before his or her name, or get lucky in the lottery that you had to register for months in advance, your only option is The Queue which is a very organized, very long line.

First, get the Tube to Wimbledon, and then take a taxi the last mile. Yes, it's only a mile, but driving past all those walking people, knowing you will be in front of them in the line, will be quite satisfying. Once you get to the grounds, be prepared to be in line for a few hours. Yes, hours! The Queue is however a fun experience. Chat with those around you, bring some food and drink, and enjoy the line as part of the whole Wimbledon experience. And, once the gates open at 10:30am, slowly, very slowly, move forward.

Important items to note.

The Queue is CASH ONLY.

As the tournament advances, the lines get longer. While arriving at 8am early in the tournament will probably get you in, on the final weekend, getting in line at 6am does not guarantee entry as they will only let people in until the grounds are full and after that only when people leave.

I know this from personal experience in 2016, when after arriving at 6:45am, and standing in line until noon, they sold out of grounds tickets 20 people in front of me. But I did get a hat, and it was quite a fun experience.

Chapter 13

There's More to the UK Than London

But what about outside the London region? York? Or Cambridge? Or Edinburgh for example? Glad you asked.

York is a fascinating city to visit. It's almost like they have built newer housing in gaps in castle walls and old towers. No, actually, that's exactly what they've done. As a result, everywhere you look, history is front and center. York Minster towers above the town, with breathtaking, well, towers and Gothic architecture that take your breath away. Nearby, the birthplace of Guy Fawkes is celebrated with the highest tribute in British culture—a pub. And if you're not familiar with Guy Fawkes, make sure you get them to tell you his story of insurrection, gunpowder, and violent death that is still celebrated every year across the UK as we all burn our 'guy' in effigy.

And speaking of pubs, let me recommend two others. One, the Chapter House, in the Principle Hotel adjacent to York train station. Also, York Tap, which is actually attached to York train station. It's not uncommon for visitors to start a pre-train drink at Chapter House, then head to the station, only to be intercepted by York Tap, putting your efficiency in making your train into a large question.

Cambridge is another treat worth visiting and spending time in. From punting along the river (and hire a punter, please don't try it yourself, no matter how easy it looks, as self-punting is only entertaining to those watching you from the land), to walking around and through Kings College Chapel, you just can't help but feel a little smarter and a little more posh when spending time in a town that has the smarts and the fun needed for a really good time. Pubs dot the landscape around town, as do shops and restaurants, and you will never run out of things to do, or photos to take.

Both cities also have significant strengths in the agritech industry, making them a great place for investment as well.

I grew up in England, but I was born in Irvine, Scotland. And every year we made a pilgrimage north of the border to my parent's hometown of Edinburgh to visit family—and to explore.

Today, living on the other side of the pond in a house bearing the name "Scotland House," my thoughts hop across the ocean far more often than I actually get to. But every visit to the capital of Scotland is a treat, no matter the time of year or the weather.

The last time I was in Edinburgh it was cold and wet. But right around the time I was starting to feel sorry for myself, I looked up and there, shining from on high, was Edinburgh Castle. And everything got better. There is something that is incredibly cool about a castle, and Edinburgh Castle is one of the best. Home of Scotland's Crown Jewels, the Stone of Destiny (on which all British monarchs are crowned) and the Royal Edinburgh Military Tattoo, it's a castle you can lose at least a day in as you experience history in person. There's also the fun story of the Stone of Destiny being stolen from Westminster Abbey in 1950, and doubt on whether the real stone was recovered.

After your day or days at the Castle, it's time for a walk down a wee hill. The Royal Mile is the road that leads down from the Castle towards the Palace of Holyroodhouse and the Scottish Parliament. It's full of stores, pubs and cafés, and surprises at every turn such as wondering what that little bookstore used to be, and discovering it was actually John Knox's house.

As you head down the Royal Mile, and if you are a Harry Potter fan, a quick side trip when you get to George IV Bridge is in order. If you're walking from the Castle, turn right on George IV Bridge, and a wee bit on your right will be The Elephant House, where JK Rowling began to create the world of wizards and wizardry. A bit beyond that will be Greyfriars Kirkyard, home of gravestones that bear the names of Thomas Riddle and William McGonagall (said to be the inspiration behind Professor McGonagall). As a side note, the nearby George Heriot's school, directly behind Greyfriars Kirkyard, is claimed to be the inspiration for Hogwarts.

A word of warning. The gravestones are in a graveyard, or cemetery as it is called in the US. So, one, respect that. Two, don't do as I did when I decided that I was actually free to go explore and find the gravestones during a very busy visit. The issue was, it was close to midnight. It took me about 20 minutes of wandering around a graveyard at midnight to realize this was probably not the smartest thing I had ever done, and it was probably best to come back when, you know, the sun was up.

For those not interested in Potter's nemesis, I still encourage a visit to learn the traditional reasons that Greyfriars Kirk is a tourist stop—Greyfriars Bobby. Greyfriars Bobby was a Sky Terrier who spent 14 years guarding the grave of its owner until the wee dog died in 1872. It is a well-known and celebrated story in Scotland that I remember from when I was a wee lad. Outside the graveyard sits a statue of Greyfriars Bobby. And of course, it is right next to the Greyfriars Bobby Bar, founded in 1873.

Now, since you are slightly off the Royal Mile, and before you continue down the hill, take a left out of Greyfriars Kirkyard on Candlemaker Row and head to Grassmarket. If it's lunchtime, there a wonderful little French restaurant called Petit Paris to enjoy. I highly recommend the lamb stew. Not in the mood for some French cuisine in the heart of Scotland? Then there are the more traditional places such as the Fiddler's Arms, The White Hart Inn (claiming to be Edinburgh's oldest pub and haunted to boot), and the Black Bull. And of course, Mamma's American Pizza.

Now you've had a wee bit of French cuisine or a few pints, it's time to continue down the Royal Mile, but make sure you take West Bow Street on your left. In my opinion, it's one of the coolest looking streets in all of Edinburgh. Then turn left on Upper Bow and right on Lawnmarket and you are back on the Royal Mile.

Now it's time to shop. Sweets (candy), souvenirs, tartan and more, it's all there on the Royal Mile. Plus, quite a number of establishments to cure your thirst so to speak.

On your way down the Royal Mile, make a quick left on Cockburn Street and you'll be standing in the location of a brilliant Avengers fight scene that started on Cockburn and ended after various individuals crashed through the roof of the Edinburgh train station.

And then at the bottom of the hill is the residence of Her Majesty—The Palace of Holyroodhouse, also known as Holyrood Palace. This is the official residence of the British Monarch in Scotland and has served as the principal residence of Kings and Queens of Scotland since the 16th century. Her Majesty spends one week in residence at the beginning of each summer, and the rest of the year the Palace is open to the public. It is worth the visit.

And behind you is the Scottish Parliament, the seat of Scotland's devolved government. Certainly something to stop in and see as they offer public tours, and you may be able to secure tickets to sit in on a debate from Tuesday through Thursday but they advise securing the debate tickets in advance.

How about a wee walk in the countryside? Yes, it is possible in Edinburgh's capital city. Edinburgh sits in a long extinct volcano system. Edinburgh Castle sits on part of it. And Arthur's Seat is the highest and largest remnant.

The peak sits in the 640-acre Royal Park adjacent to Holyrood Palace and is also the site of a large and well-preserved fort. It is a walk up a hill, so sturdy footwear is recommended and watch out for slippery surfaces and sheer drops. But the view is absolutely worth it.

On the other side of Edinburgh Castle from Arthur's Seat is Princes Street, part of the newer part of Edinburgh, built in stages from 1767 to 1850. This is home to lots of shopping, some beautiful gardens below the Castle, and the Scott Monument. Additionally, if you happen to be there in late November or December, the entire area is lit up for

Christmas, and a huge Christmas Market takes over the area along with many other attractions that pop up for the season.

Time for a break? Then take advantage of my favorite Starbucks location in the world. Located at 120 Princes Street, this second-floor location offers a lovely cuppa, plus phenomenal views of Edinburgh Castle. Don't be fooled by the ground floor to-go counter. Just walk past it to head up the stairs and relax for a wee bit.

And now, it's time for some haggis. If you want to take a bus ride or an Uber, I recommend St. Andrews restaurant in Portobello. I love their haggis and chips and they even have gluten-free fish and chips. St. Andrews has been around since 1920 and has built a reputation as the best fish and chips in Scotland. I can't argue with that.

However, if you want to stay closer to central Edinburgh, then head to the west end of Princes Street, and nip into Ryrie's, an establishment that's been around since the 1800s. My choice of food and drink? The Ryrie's Burger (Buccleuch beef burger topped with haggis, topped with burger, topped with haggis) and a Tennant's. However, if that's not your cup of tea, there's also haddock and chips, steak pie, bangers and mash, and much more. Combine that with an extensive selection of Scottish drafts and whisky and you're set for a fine evening. I've heard they also offer salad, but why?

And now it is time to head out from central Edinburgh in one of two directions for a wee bit of footie. Edinburgh is home to two football teams, Heart of Midlothian (Hearts) to the southwest at Tynecastle, and Hibernian (Hibs) to the northeast at Easter Road. Both are in the Scottish Premier League, and both are fun matches to watch. Hearts and Hibs play each other a few times a year, but even if you can't catch them together, taking in one or both is well worth the time. However, a warning, sometimes (aka most of the time) Scottish football is not a friendly place for wee ears if that's a concern for you. And if the home team decides to fall apart, threats towards one's own players are not abnormal from the stands. Ahh, Scotland!

From a business sense, Scottish Development International is a great resource to rely on for insights and information you need as you evaluate whether Scotland might make more sense for your American business over England, or Wales, or Northern Ireland.

And speaking of America.

Chapter 14

Discovering America Between the Coasts

Many Brits are familiar with Florida, New York, California and maybe Chicago. And these are all fun to visit, and I have done so many times. The rest of the USA however, especially the section in the middle, is a mystery to many internationals.

Needless to say, there is much to see in America. From the National Churchill Museum in Fulton, Missouri, to the steam railroad through the mountains near Mt. Rushmore in South Dakota, to the mountains of Colorado, and everything between and throughout.

My thoughts are that we should all get beyond what you hear about on TV and do some exploring. Rent an RV and drive across country. Spend a week on a small island between Destin and Pensacola, Florida, called Navarre. And stop in to Pensacola to see the US Navy Blue Angels demonstration team practice.

Enjoy the craft beer scene in Missouri, or even the wine scene which is top notch. But get out there. Enjoy the people. Enjoy the food and drink. Enjoy the culture.

Some of my favorite places to visit include Kansas City, Missouri and the Lake of the Ozarks, also in Missouri. In fact, the Big Cedar Lodge is luxury in the midst of nature. Amazing golf, outdoor activities, boating, fishing, shooting, horse riding, and some of the best accommodations. St. Louis is phenomenal for craft beer and wine, with my favorite wine area being in the hills of Augusta, Missouri.

Outside of Missouri, you'll find me in the panhandle of Florida, or up in Chicago, or in West Palm Beach. Washington DC is also a favorite place to visit, with great food and great history everywhere.

On the west coast, I enjoy Imperial Beach and La Hoja, along with Santa Barbara—the American Riviera.

If American sports is your focus, you actually don't need to go far beyond Missouri. Missouri is home to the St. Louis Cardinals and the Kansas City Royals, if baseball is your interest. If American Football, then the Kansas City Chiefs is an amazing experience in one of the loudest stadiums in the country. Ice hockey? Back to St. Louis with the St. Louis Blues. Major League Soccer? Just across the Missouri border into Kansas gets you Sporting Kansas City, or you can head up to Chicago for the Chicago Fire Soccer Club.

Looking for a river cruise of a different sort than you would find in Europe? Then take a cruise on a luxury riverboat along the Mississippi, making sure to stop in at Hannibal, Missouri—the hometown of Mark Twain.

Into motorcycles? Then Route 66 is a fun ride, taking you through the heart of America at a pace that will ensure you meet some amazing people across the country. You'll also see huge rocking chairs and small-town culture. And you can make slight detours along the way to places like Branson, Missouri, known as the "live entertainment capital of the world," or the Grand Canyon and Meteor Crater in Arizona.

And then there's the train. A good friend of mine recently took the train from Chicago to Seattle via Wisconsin, Minnesota, North Dakota, Montana and Idaho. If you want to see the desolate beauty that exists in the northern USA this is a great way to take 3 days to enjoy a relaxed tour where someone else is doing the "driving" and you have the privacy of your own cabin.

Bottom line. Get out. Explore. Meet people. And enjoy the diversity and the welcoming attitude that is present in most of America.

So, now you've tolerated my love for the United Kingdom and its food, culture and more, and been inspired to hit the road in America, let's get back to more serious topics.

Darts.

Chapter 15
Picking a Landing Spot

Well, hopefully not darts actually. But, after looking at a map of America, and thinking about holiday or vacation spots, you might just be considering tossing a metal projectile at something as you try to decide where to enter the US market. And vice versa, Scotland, England, Yorkshire, Hampshire, Farnborough, Glasgow? Where to start? And what's the difference?

People buy what they know. It's a common thing in marketing. You want people to know and identify with your brand, so that they are comfortable parting with their hard-earned money for your products.

The same is true for companies investing in the UK and the US. If you know London, you are more inclined to pursue starting your UK presence there. If you know New York, or Los Angeles, or Houston, then by golly those are where we should start our new venture into the US.

Stop. Wait a minute. It is entirely possible that one of those choices is perfect for you. However, it is entirely possible that none of them are, and by choosing what are some of the more expensive places to do business and ones that are on one edge of America or in a part of the UK where space is lacking and talent attraction is highly competitive, you may be destroying your success before you have any.

In the US, there are 50 states. In the UK, there are four countries. Each state or country is different in taxes, regulations, insurance rules, banking rules, costs of doing business, talent availability, support structure in the communities and regionally, and in many other ways.

Missouri for example is about to lower its corporate income tax rate to 4 percent, making it the second lowest rate in the US among states that collect corporate income tax. Other states might not have corporate income tax. But states might also have higher fees in other areas or not be stable with their energy costs. Or the infrastructure in place might be great or awful for your business.

Missouri for example has every Class 1 railroad in America coming to it, and the Mississippi River provides ice-free, lock-and-dam-free access to the Gulf of Mexico year-round. But if you're looking for a state that is going to incentivize solar farms and that are a prime location for solar energy production, then another state might be better (although I do contend Missouri is a leader in developing energy storage technology thanks to companies like Eagle Picher, who just happen to power the International Space Station and every Mars mission).

Making the right choice on a location is probably the most important decision you will make if you are investing and starting up a new facility across the Pond.

So where to start? Who can help?

For a US company, looking to invest in the UK, you should chat with the Department of International Trade (DIT) at your local British Consulate. Also, in some of those consulates are experts on Wales, Northern Ireland and Scotland, such as Scottish Development International.

The team at the US Embassy in London can also assist. As can attorneys, accountants, investment bankers, trade associations and chambers, and regional groups such as London and Partners.

For UK companies looking at the US, the list is all of the above, plus state level organizations such as Missouri Partnership or Enterprise Florida. Professional site selectors or location advisors are also a premium addition to any team looking to expand in the US. I also highly recommend the SelectUSA Investment Summit held each summer in Washington DC. At this event you will quickly meet representatives from many US states and regions, all of whom should be able to deliver detailed insights into what investing in their part of America looks like, including cost breakdowns, available locations and incentives, within a couple of weeks.

"I think American companies are always surprised at the employment regulations in the UK," says James Cummings with London and Partners. "It's a lot friendlier than mainland Europe, but I think they are really surprised about how much notice you have to give in the UK."

Yes, regulations in the UK are rather different from the US. Many parts of the US are "at will" when it comes to employment. Two weeks' notice in these parts of the world are almost just a courtesy, and usually the only repercussions if you don't give two weeks' notice is the lack of a recommendation in the future. And for a US person in the UK, the idea that you have to give anything more than two weeks is almost an alien concept to them.

There are also holidays (or vacations as they say in America). Many American companies setting up shop in the UK are shocked by how much holiday people receive. Also, health care. Senior executives will probably expect private health care. The rest of the employees utilize the public system. A US company, walking into the UK, could make the rather expensive mistake of simply providing private insurance to all employees, like they do in the US.

Another element of investing in the UK that US companies are surprised by, according to Cummings, is just how different England, Scotland, Wales and Northern Ireland are from each other.

"Broadly, it's the same employment regulations," he says. But there are advantages and disadvantages of different parts of the UK depending on your company needs, your industry, your talent needs, your tax and regulatory implications, and more.

Financial services is a sector where London is leading the way, globally. But even when you are in The City you are only a twenty-minute taxi ride from the UK Government and Whitehall.

Agtech and life science are more outside of London with strong segments in Cambridge and Oxford, further north in York and across the border into Scotland.

And in both countries, politicians are not the best resource. Apologies to my many friends in politics on both sides of the Pond, but their plates are full, and you won't get the deep level of support needed to empower your investment, and to give you the best odds of success.

But certainly, invite them all to the ribbon cutting or chat with them when some onerous regulation is stifling innovation in your area of focus.

"I would say New York has even more of a snappy, straight-down-to-business approach, whereas other areas can be a bit more about getting to know your counterpart first, over coffee or a meal," a senior British diplomat mentioned when we were talking recently. "I have had southerners in the US say they think they benefit from being under-estimated when they come up to NYC for business negotiations. And there are places in the US where I am sure it matters more than in NYC how long you have been part of the local community and how well plugged in to the local area you are."

And that is key when investing in the US. Most states are not going to throw money at you when you are considering investing there. Missouri for example offers some great incentives, but they are usually directly tied to jobs created. You have to earn them. Now, you can get local tax abatements and other tax credits, but the local community has got to want to give them to you. So building that solid relationship as you are evaluating a community is key because the community is also evaluating you.

A contact, and a keen economic mind, at the UK Embassy in Washington, DC, gave me this advice. "There are lots of differences across the country," he said. "People looking to do business in the US should do some research into the region they are visiting. It will pay dividends in the long run." I could not agree more.

My friend at Scottish Development International took it even further. "Each state is different from the next," he said. "Each government has different priorities, regulations, and laws, which in turn affect what industries and/or products will thrive in that given region. Look at renewable energy and low-carbon technologies—companies wouldn't want to simply do business in the US; they'd want to do business in California (solar) or New York (energy systems technologies) or Texas (onshore wind) depending on their respective strengths."

When looking at the UK from the US, some advice I received is that outside the southeast of England it may be more like outside of NYC and the northeast in the US, meaning a slightly warmer welcome and greater willingness to take time to build connections. It is also important for American businesses to be aware that the nations of Scotland, Northern Ireland and Wales are all fiercely proud and patriotic. In England you will find that people are very proud of the city/region they come from, and in Scotland, Wales and Northern Ireland being a part of that respective country is a huge identity for them. And remember, England,

Scotland, Wales and Northern Ireland are in fact countries in their own right and identity, within the country of the United Kingdom.

Americans also assume that Scotland and the UK are bigger geographically than they are. It helps to understand just how easy it is to get across the UK, and that Glasgow and Edinburgh, for instance, are only 45 minutes apart by train. Recently, I took a business delegation from London to York for just one day. It was a 2.5-hour train ride each way, and it was a full day, but it was an easy trip for Americans who are used to day trips from St. Louis into DC or Chicago for business reasons.

On the other hand, British companies tend to underestimate the diversity of economies within the US. It's always an important lesson to learn that the United States essentially comprises 50 individual economies with varying policies, regulations, and political environments. Once this mental shift is made, UK companies tend to focus on priority markets and succeed at a much higher pace.

My friend at SDI also stressed that, "Scotland has a great reputation amongst businesses due to the support that is made available by SDI and the Scottish Government, whether that be in the form of financial assistance or logistical support such as account management, recruitment consulting, property search assistance, and so on. Scotland continually ranks as the best place for foreign direct investment in the UK, outside of London, and this is due in large part to the talent, university cluster, quality of life, and cost effectiveness."

I would also argue that each individual country within the United Kingdom can claim some measure of significant support for companies investing and creating jobs there.

Amit Kothari, the British CEO of the software company Tallyfy who chose Missouri as their landing spot in North America, had some additional advice on, well, advice.

"We would have sought advice from great people in our space earlier," he said when asked what he would have done differently. "And we would have been more aggressive on a niche pitch for paid pilots."

"We were very new to St. Louis in particular," he said. "Winning an Arch Grant was by far the most transformative experience for us. It not only brought us to St. Louis, but it also introduced us to a social and business ecosystem that we value greatly." Arch Grants are $50,000 non-equity investments in startups that establish a presence in St. Louis.

As for lessons learned? "Sometimes knowing what not to do as a product company is very important," Amit said. "It's a lesson learned early in our evolution."

And of course, I couldn't let him go without asking him why he chose the same US city I did to live and work.

"The cost of living is much lower than the coasts, there's easy, productive and fast access to business people and advice, there's real applicability for innovative products to many companies in the region, and there's fantastic talent."

I cannot help but agree with all of that.

Chapter 16

Launching Your Brand

Jack Irvine has just a wee bit of experience with US companies entering the UK and vice versa. As a former reporter and a long-time public affairs leader, he has worked with numerous CEOs and Chairmen around the world, and regularly advises senior leaders on market entry and how to be a disruptor when you do so.

When I chatted with him recently as he sat in the London office of Media House International, the firm he launched in 1991, the insights were plentiful.

Usually when you launch a product in the UK, the product is front and center, he told me. However, with an American beverage product he is currently launching, they are actually embracing the in-your-face American persona, and already seeing some success.

"The guy is a real go-getter," Jack said. "He is going to disrupt the market with this approach. The product is great. The CEO is incredibly smart."

But it didn't go smoothly at first. The American CEO first came to the UK and signed up with a distributor and a PR company and everything was going swimmingly. Until the PR company decided to issue a press release, an un-approved press release, that tied the product to a political issue of the day. The distributor dropped the American company like a hot potato, and everything looked like it was over.

And then Jack got involved. As someone with years of experience supporting American companies in the UK, and with his vast network of connections, he introduced the company to a new distributor, took over their PR efforts, and helped them build the right support team in the UK.

"The American guy was coming into an alien culture, was let down by the wrong partners, and had trouble with a legal firm in London that didn't approach things how he would expect," Jack shared. "It proves that if you are an American coming into Britain, it's all very well to have a lawyer and an accountant, but you need incredibly strong connections in country in order to cut through all the crap."

And it goes both directions. The same is true as you look to enter the US. And Jack stressed the importance of shopping around to find the best members of your team.

"A good American is fantastic," Jack said. "A good Brit is fantastic. You just may need to shop around to find good people in both countries. Try to get to know somebody who knows the best possible people for you and the best possible location."

Americans also like the precise way that Brits write and communicate. Looking back on his days as a journalist, Jack describes it as, "The Brits get the story in the first paragraph and then explain it. The Americans get the story in the 20th paragraph." And writing skills between the two countries are very different. "As a Brit in America, they might appreciate your concise style, however you may need to adapt slightly to local preferences."

Be creative. He shared one story of a Scottish manufacturer who served US customers at the time US manufacturing was converting to just-in-time production. His US customers wanted him to set up a manufacturing facility in the US, to ensure the product was at the plant at exactly the right moment. So, with Scottish ingenuity, the CEO moved to Chicago, set up an office and everything that goes into that, and then partnered with the airlines to ship his product from Scotland to the US at exactly the moments he needed them. And continued to do this for years to come.

The key to his success was his willingness to "live" in the new market for a while, until the system got off the ground. That's exactly what the current CEO that Jack is working with is doing. For six months, the CEO and his family are living in London, and blitzing the market. And engaging with their customers in person. And, of course, selling a quality product that has a genuine story and a real-world impact.

"Whether you're speaking to a UK audience or whether they're speaking to us, you're still just who you are," Aaron Perlut, founder of the US marketing firm Elasticity, said. "Your story is part of your value proposition. Asides from just solving a problem, you need to link your brand and your backstory to how you solved the problem and then you focus in on the product."

Aaron stresses the importance of being authentic in how you present yourself, and clearly show what problem you solve with your product. He touted Square and My Pillow as examples of brands that clearly show the problem and then the solution for the problem.

Mike Lindell, the creator and face of My Pillow, talks about the problem of bad pillows, how they cause bad sleep, and then he tosses in some medical stats about good pillows leading to better sleep, which can lead to more effectiveness as a human being and more productivity.

"In one fell swoop he takes the problem, creates the solution, ties it to benefits for you, and ends with 'I know it works because it helped me,'" Aaron said. "It made them a household name."

"Square came out of a problem that Jim McKelvey, Square's cofounder, had when selling blown glass in his hometown of St. Louis, Missouri," Aaron continued. "He would go to shows to sell his glass pieces, but no one ever had five to seven hundred dollars in their pockets. And Jim realized, if he could take a credit card from just about anyone using a smart phone, he could solve this problem for a lot of people. He did, he told that story, and the brand has become a global point-of-sale product."

Another point Aaron stressed was the value in making your product experiential as you market it.

"Red Bull does experiential marketing on multiple fronts," he said. "If you're at a sporting event there is about a 50-50 chance you're going to see a Mini, driven by two attractive women, giving out free Red Bull. And it's like shooting fish in a barrel, because they are looking for hyper-active males, and they are giving them product and creating brand affinity."

Red Bull also creates events for thrill seekers that are then shared online. "They are creating experiences that really identify with the people they have identified as the consumers of their product," Aaron shared. "They know their audience, which is mostly young and active on digital. And they do a tremendous job creating high-quality content that appeals to the sensibilities of young men."

And then add to your authenticity and your experiential approach with a little bit of disruptive.

"Whenever I say the word 'disruptive' I always have to add the caveat that it doesn't have to mean doing something ridiculous or silly. It could be sad. It could be heartwarming. We are so inundated with information and content all the time so that disruption—breaking through the clutter—is essential."

The final point to stress as you launch your brand or new product in a new market is the ability to target your messages to where your desired audience actually consumes their information or where they would be most influenced to purchase your product.

"If it's a beer brand, then putting advertising on urinals at a sports venue might be great for you," Aaron suggested. "I'm already out of the game, so I might as well buy a beer on the way back in. And, by the way, that beer is situated right outside this urinal stand. So, awareness and proximity are both important."

Geofencing with digital is also a powerful tool, as is customizing content for your audience on their preferred online channels and communicating in the way they like to be communicated to.

"For instance, if you're speaking to teen girls, they are on Snapchat and on Instagram," Aaron said. "But they are certainly not on Facebook watching three-minute videos as that's where they perceive their parents and grandparents to be. And then once you are in those channels, communicating in the style your target audience prefers, getting back to the authenticity of your story is really important."

"People want to do business with people they trust."

Chapter 17
Brexit and Free Trade

On June 23, 2016, the British people went to the polls after then Prime Minister David Cameron decided to ask a key question on the future of the UK, "Should the United Kingdom remain a member of the European Union or leave the European Union?"

Seventy two percent of the UK's registered voters showed up with an opinion, and after all 33 million had cast their votes, the UK basically said, in Monty Python fashion, "and now it's time for something completely different." Yes, the British people voted to leave the European Union (EU). But next up was the question of what that actually looks like.

Great question.

The following three years saw the triggering of Article 50, which started a two-ish year "leaving the EU" countdown for the UK with negotiations between the UK and the EU taking the world on a rollercoaster of headlines and emotional reactions. This countdown was originally planned to end on March 29, 2019 but that didn't quite happen. The date got shifted, the negotiations continued, another Prime Minister stepped down and the world wondered what the final deal would look like.

But here's what is important. I said this the day after the referendum, and I have continued to believe it throughout the process. The UK will be fine. It's the fifth largest economy in the world, and the world, including the EU, wants to trade with the UK. To put that in a US perspective, the UK economy is larger than California's. Now, with any economic change there is always pain and opportunity, but I believe the pain will be short-term, and the opportunity will be great.

I also don't agree with the pain points that many in the media are claiming. I don't expect food shortages. I don't expect the fleeing of companies from the UK, although there will be some (while at the same time new companies expand into the UK for the first time or the fifth time). You will also have companies who are making cuts or changes that choose to blame Brexit, even though Brexit has nothing to do with their decision. I only hope that this tactic is only used by a minimal number of companies.

In fact, on the food topic, a British-American friend of mine who founded the British Monarchist Society decided to take a tour of his local shops in London to see just how much fresh produce from the EU was at risk of disappearing from the shelves. And, apparently, it's already happened as of 2018. He could not find a single piece of fresh fruit or vegetable that was from the EU. There was lots of food from Mexico and Peru and other southern hemisphere countries, but nothing from the EU.

After additional conversations with others, including another friend who is involved in the supply chain for a nationwide chain of stores in the UK that, among many things, sells packaged and fresh food, apparently food only comes from the EU during the summer, and, in his opinion, it would be easy to replace those products with products from countries outside of the EU, like the US. The key, of course, is rapidly negotiating trade deals with all these countries to allow the continued free flow of goods into and out of the UK.

And there comes the opportunity. For British companies who are feeling a little nervous about their flow of goods into the EU, might I suggest that America would be a good destination for your products. And for American companies, now is the time to find out if your products can fill a need in the UK that has been filled by EU products up to this point.

President Trump has, well, trumpeted his intention to increase the flow of trade between our two countries. On February 15, 2019, the President, during comments in the Rose Garden, talked about increasing trade substantially via a US-UK trade deal and that it would be great for jobs and prosperity for both nations. US Ambassador to the UK Woody Johnson tweeted on March 1 that, "We are ready to strike the most ambitious, comprehensive trade deal in the history of the Special Relationship. Free, fair & reciprocal trade [equals] more jobs & prosperity on both sides of the Atlantic."

Prior to that tweet, on February 26, Ambassador Johnson tweeted, "President Trump, Congress and the London Embassy—we're all committed to working with UK Parliamentarians to secure a future free trade agreement!"

On March 14, President Trump himself tweeted, "My administration looks forward to negotiating a large-scale Trade Deal with the United Kingdom. The potential is unlimited!"

And that sentiment has continued, with US leadership tweeting on a regular basis that the US is ready for a trade deal and that the UK will be in the front of the queue when it comes to getting one done.

But, to the outsider looking in via the variety of media coverage, it looks like chaos. It isn't, but there are so many divergent groups and opinions involved that it can easily seem that way. But I would encourage you to step back and look beyond what is taking place or allegedly taking place in the halls of Westminster.

Another friend of mine, Simon Constable, whom I had the privilege of getting to know when he was at the Wall Street Journal and who now writes for a number of outlets and is a fellow at the Johns Hopkins Institute for Applied Economics, Global Health and the Study of Business Enterprise, put it incredibly well in his March 21 *Forbes* article.

"By most economic measures Britain's economy is performing far better than comparable economies across the channel in mainland Europe," he writes. "The UK economy has a far lower unemployment rate than that of the eurozone, the EU's single currency area. In Britain, it recently dipped to yet another multi-decade low of 3.9%, according to data collated by statistics website Trading Economics. Compare that to the eurozone which has an unemployment rate of 7.8%, with higher rates of 10.5% and 8.8% in Italy and France respectively."

And then he adds more data and facts to the argument.

"Economic growth in the UK is modest, but it still beats its major rivals on the continent," Simon claims. "The UK grew at an annualized rate of 1.3% in the latest period measured compared to 1.1% for the entire eurozone. It was far worse in Italy, France, and Germany which had zero growth, 0.9%, and 0.6% respectively."

"Put simply, in terms of economic vibrancy Britain is hands down beating the other large economies of Europe, such as Germany, France, and Italy."

I am convinced that this positive performance will continue post-Brexit or whatever comes from this process we are experiencing. Yes, there will be some short-term pain in places. There always is when national and international economics change. But there will also be great opportunity coming off the back of a solid track record of performance and growth.

Simon is equally as insightful when it comes to looking at the US under a Trump administration. Back in February 2017, Simon, in another Forbes piece, took us on a deep dive into the Global Economic Policy Uncertainty Index. This index tracks global economic news and happenings and charts them. When he wrote in February 2017, the global uncertainty levels were at record highs. The US, not so much. Fast forward to February 2019 and we find the global index only slightly below that record peak in 2017, and December 2018 was another global record high for uncertainty. Today, the US uncertainty level is significantly lower than it was in February 2017.

Bottom line, the US economic uncertainty levels are at about where historic averages have been, going all the way back to 1998. The world however is at record high levels of economic uncertainty.

In today's global economy, the US is a safe business bet.

And, an interesting side note is that the UK is equally as average on the uncertainty index. Admittedly slightly above average, but not that far above. And far below the peak it hit in July 2016 immediately following the Brexit vote and far below the global levels of uncertainty.

Here's what I want you to remember, if nothing else. There is significant opportunity for British companies looking to expand to the North American market via the Midwest, and Missouri in particular. And there are significant opportunities for US companies looking to expand into the UK and Europe in various places within the British Isles.

Regardless of where Brexit takes the UK, the fundamentals do not change. Hard Brexit = opportunity for increased trade and investment. Negotiated Brexit = opportunity for increased trade and investment. No Brexit = yes, you guessed it, opportunity for increased trade and investment. The fact that the UK and the US have a special relationship does not change. The opportunities in each country may shift or adjust based on what happens with

Brexit, but the fact remains that the opportunities are plentiful and attractive.

And have a plan, a team, and advisors or experts to help you along the way. Business development, like economic development, is a team sport.

Oh, and if you still think the US and the UK are the same after reading all this, consider me gobsmacked and of the opinion that your cross-Pond business plans might be a wee bit dodgy or at the very least, quite daft.

Go ye therefore, and invest across the Pond!

About the Author

Mark Sutherland was born at a very young age in Irvine, Scotland, lived for a wee bit in Edinburgh, and was then dragged, kicking and screaming, into England—much to the annoyance of the gentleman in the plane seat in front of 1-year old Mark.

In England, he fell in love with his new home, and grew to appreciate all of the United Kingdom. Its history, its food, its people and its opportunity.

In the late 80s, Mark emigrated to the US, and landed in Missouri, home of a big Arch, and welcoming people. He's been in Missouri ever since, working in marketing, economic development and public relations, launching businesses, falling in love, raising a family, and bragging about Missouri globally.

During this time, he was also appointed as the British Honorary Consul to Missouri representing British diplomatic and economic interests statewide, and as a GlobalScot which is a group of around 600 business leaders globally appointed by Scotland's First Minister to assist Scottish companies as they grow globally and to assist overseas companies as they look to invest in Scotland. Mark graduated from Washington University in St. Louis with a global business degree, has received volunteer awards from two U.S. presidents, plays around with kilts and jets (not at the same time thank goodness), and is a regular on radio and television due to the fact that Yanks like British accents—a lot.

Today he continues a long-term vision of bringing Missouri and the United Kingdom closer together and recruits people on both sides of the Pond to assist.

He proudly claims to have three home countries.

You can connect with Mark via LinkedIn at linkedin.com/in/markisutherland/ or follow him on Twitter at twitter.com/markisutherland and Instagram at instagram.com/markisutherland/.

Acknowledgements

Where do you start as you look back on 30 years of people who have supported you?

You start with your better half. My support. My cheerleader. My encourager. My amazing wife Amy. Thank you for all you do, and all you put up with, as I dream of making a difference in the world, and specifically in the connections between the UK and the US. I could not do any of this without you by my side.

To my parents. A son could not have better role models and examples. You have given me a love for my home country, my second home country and my new home country.

To my kids. Who hate it when I go out of town, but still think what I do is cool. And who make me feel loved when I return.

To the bosses who became my friends and who encouraged me to pursue this dream, and supported me practically in that endeavor—Glynn, Aaron, Hugh, Subash and Steve. To have a boss who sees the value in what you are doing, even though it may not perfectly fit within your day job, and to support it in every way, is an amazing thing.

To my friends and colleagues who have dreamed with me, supported me, and who are doing great things with me and without me that will have impact for generations. John and Gina, Gordon and Kelley, Derek and Ashley, Alan and Jodi, Jerry and Cindy, Ally, Garrett, Paul, Chris, Phil and Laura, Ed, and many more.

To my friends who have chosen to serve in Her Majesty's Government, in the Scottish Government and in governments across the US in support of a cause and a vision bigger than themselves, and who have chosen to partner with me in this mission. Steve, John, Charlie, Mark, Kyle, Ross, Martin, Derek, Donnie, Hart, Lord Paul, Haydn, Rob, Kate, Brandon and a number of others.

To the many people I have worked alongside over the years who have a shared passion for a stronger special relationship between the UK and the US. And to just a few of those who were great sounding boards for the content of this book, and insightful in ways that you, the reader, will reap the benefits from. Jim, Brandon, Richard, Ross, Jim, Amit, John, Chris, James and Simon. Thank you for your work, your vision, and your dedication.

Appendix A
Useful Organizations

Investing in the USA

SelectUSA – bit.ly/PB-SelectUSA

U.S. Embassy in London – bit.ly/PB-USA

Missouri Partnership – bit.ly/PB-MOPartnership

AllianceSTL – bit.ly/PB-AllianceSTL

KCADC – bit.ly/PB-KCADC

Springfield Regional Economic Partnership – bit.ly/PB-Springfield

Missouri Economic Development Council – bit.ly/PB-MEDC

Missouri Department of Economic Development – bit.ly/PB-MODED

Missouri Technology Corporation – bit.ly/PB-MTC

Accelerate St. Louis – bit.ly/PB-ASTL

Arch Grants – bit.ly/PB-ArchGrants

BioGenerator – bit.ly/PB-Bio

BioSTL – bit.ly/PB-BioSTL

SixThirty – bit.ly/PB-630

SixThirty CYBER – bit.ly/PB-630CYBER

YieldLab – bit.ly/PB-YL

Note: Most states have similar organizations to the Missouri organizations listed that are focused on assisting companies looking to invest in their region of the US.

Investing in the UK

Department for International Trade – bit.ly/PB-DIT

Scottish Development International – bit.ly/PB-SDI

This is Wales – bit.ly/PB-Wales

Invest Northern Ireland – bit.ly/PB-NI

London and Partners – bit.ly/PB-LandP

Agri-Tech East – bit.ly/PB-AgriTechEast

UK Angel Investment Network – bit.ly/PB-UKAngel

The LEP Network - bit.ly/PB-LEP

UK Trade Associations - bit.ly/PB-TradeAssociations

Consulting Firms - bit.ly/PB-Firms

Appendix B

Code Words – The Complete-ish List

Anorak: a hooded coat (parka) or a socially impaired obsessive
Answerphone: an automated telephone-answering machine
Anti-clockwise: counterclockwise
Approved school: a reform school for juvenile delinquents
Articulated lorry: semi-truck
Aubergine: eggplant
Auntie or Auntie Beeb: affectionate term for the BBC
Autocue: teleprompter
Barmaid or barman: bartender
Barmy: crazy, unbalanced or balmy
Barney: noisy quarrel or trouble
Barrister: In England, Wales, and Northern Ireland, this used to be the only type of lawyer qualified to argue a case in both higher and lower law courts; contrasts with solicitor. For Scotland, the term is advocate. Occasionally used in the U.S., but not to define any particular type of lawyer.
Bedsit: one-room flat with shared bathroom facilities
Bespoke: custom-made to a buyer's specification
Bevvy: alcoholic beverage
Biro: ballpoint pen.
Biscuit (UK): cookie (US)
Blimey: exclamation of surprise.
Bloke: dude
Blower: telephone
Bobby: police officer
Bodge: cheap or poor (repair) job

Boffin: expert, such as a scientist or engineer
Bonnet: hood of a car
Brolly: umbrella
Bunce: windfall, profit or bonus
Caravan park: trailer park or RV park
Car boot: trunk of the car
Car hire: car rental
Car park: parking lot or parking garage
Cash machine: ATM
Chartered Accountant: Certified Public Accountant
Cheerio: exclamation of farewell
Chips (UK): french fries (US)
Chips (US): crisps (UK)
Chuffed: proud, satisfied or pleased.
Clingfilm: plastic wrap or Saran wrap
Codswallop: "you're talking garbage"
Cor blimey: exclamation of surprise
Counterfoil: stub of a cheque or ticket
Cuppa: cup of tea (never coffee or another beverage)
Current account: checking account
Curriculum vitae: resumé
Daft: odd, mad or eccentric
Doddle: something easily accomplished
Dodgy: unsound, unstable, unreliable or sketchy
Dole: welfare
Donkey's years: a very long time
Dosh: money (US dough)
Drawing pin: thumbtack
Dual carriageway: divided highway
Dustbin: a trash can or wastebasket
Economy class: coach class
Elastoplast: Band-Aid
Engaged tone: a telephone busy signal
Estate agent: realtor
Estate car: station wagon
Ex-directory: unlisted phone number
Fairy cake: cupcake
Fairy lights: Christmas lights
First Floor: ground floor in the UK. The floor above the ground floor in the US.

Fiscal: short for procurator fiscal, name of the public prosecutor in Scotland
Flyover: road overpass
Footie or football: soccer
Fortnight: two weeks
Full stop: US period punctuation mark
Gangway: aisle
Gearbox: car transmission
Gherkin: pickle
Gob: mouth
Gobsmacked: utterly astonished or open-mouthed
Gor blimey: exclamation of surprise
Gormless: stupid or clumsy
Go-slow: protest in which workers deliberately work slowly
Greengrocer: retail trader in fruit and vegetables
Grotty: disgusting, dirty or of poor quality
Gumption: initiative, common sense, or courage
Gutties or trainers: tennis shoes
Hash sign: the symbol "#" (US number sign, pound sign or hash tag)
High street: main street
Hire: to rent
Hoarding: billboard
Hold-all: duffel bag
Hoover: vacuum cleaner
Inverted commas: quotation marks
Jacket potato: baked potato
Jiggery-pokery: trickery or dishonest behavior
Jumper: a sweater
Jump leads: jumper cables
Kitchen roll: paper towels
Knackered: exhausted
Knickers: panties
Loo: toilet or bathroom
Lorry: truck
Maths: mathematics
MD: managing director or CEO
Motorway: freeway or Interstate Highway
Nappy: diaper
NHS: National Health Service
Newsagent: convenience store

Nice one: a way of thanking or congratulating someone
Nick: to steal
Nosh: food or meal
Number plate: car license plate
OAP: Old Age Pensioner or senior citizen
Off-licence: liquor store
Off-the-peg: off-the-rack
Off you/we go: let's go
Overleaf: on the other side or reverse side of the page
P45: a pink slip
Paraffin: kerosene
Paracetamol: similar to acetaminophen
Pear-shaped: to go drastically or dramatically wrong
Pelican crossing: pedestrian crossing with lights
People mover or people carrier: minivan
Petrol: gasoline
Pitch: playing field
Plain flour: all-purpose flour
Plait: braid, as in hair
Plaster: Band-Aid
Plasterboard: drywall
Plimsoll: tennis shoe
Postage and packing: shipping and handling, S&H
Postal order: a money order
Postbox: mail box
Postcode: ZIP code
Pound shop: dollar store
Pram: baby carriage
Pub: bar
Puncture: flat tire
Pushbike: bicycle
Pushchair: baby stroller
Quid: pound sterling
Queue: line of people
Retail park: strip mall
Return: round-trip ticket.
Rubbish: trash or garbage
Rucksack: backpack.
Sat nav: GPS
Sellotape: Scotch tape
Shopping trolley: shopping cart

Sixes and sevens: crazy or muddled
Skip: dumpster
Sleeping partner: silent business partner
Slip road: entrance and exit ramps
Smart dress: formal attire
Solicitor: attorney
Spanner: wrench
Spotted dick: English steamed suet pudding containing dried fruit
Squidgy: squishy
Stockist: retailer or dealer
Straight away: immediately
Sun cream: sunscreen
Swot: to study or cram for an exam
Sweets: candy
Swimming costume: swimsuit
Ta: thank you in Scotland
Takeaway: takeout food
Takings: receipts of money at a shop
Tea towel: dish towel
Telly: television
Tenner: ten-pound note
Tipping down: raining hard
Toad-in-the-hole: batter-baked sausages
Trainers: sneakers
Transit van: generic name for a full-size panel van
Turn-indicator: turn signal
Uni: short for university
Wage packet: paycheck
WC: bathroom or restroom
Wellies: rubber boots
White coffee: coffee with milk or cream.
White pudding: oat and fat sausage
Windscreen: windshield
Write-off: total loss
Zebra crossing: crosswalk